Happy 81st!
We thought of you when
we read the marvelous
descriptions of God's
creatures. We hope you
enjoy it.
                We love you Pa!
        Dan and Cheri

The Evolution of a Creationist

The

Evolution of a *Creationist*

by Dr. Jobe Martin

A LAYMEN'S GUIDE

to the conflict between

THE BIBLE

AND

EVOLUTIONARY THEORY

Biblical Discipleship Publishers
Rockwall, Texas

Published by
Biblical Discipleship Publishers
2212 Chisholm Trail
Rockwall, Texas   75087

Library of Congress Cataloging-in-Publication Data

Martin, Jobe R.   1940 -
   The Evolution of a Creationist

   214 p. cm.
   ISBN 0-9643665-0-9
   1. Religion - Christian. 2. Creation Science.
   3. Creation/Evolution debate. 4. Christian Gospel

I. Title   II. Title: A Layman's Guide to the Conflict Between
the Bible and Evolutionary Theory

All Scripture quotations in this book are taken from the King
James version of the Bible.

Printed in the United States of America

This book is dedicated to my
Creator and Savior, the Lord Jesus Christ
To God alone be the glory.
(Rev. 4:11)

*All who gave of their time
and talents in producing this book
did so by God's grace and for His eternal glory,
for our sufficiency comes from God
(2 Corinthians 3:5),
and without Him we can do nothing.
(John 15:5b).*

TABLE OF
Contents

PREFACE

This book is a condensation and simplification of more than twenty years of studies that moved me from unquestioning belief in Darwinian evolution to undoubting trust in the special six-day creation by God as presented in the Biblical account.

It is my conviction that a simple discussion of the major questions in the creation/evolution controversy is needed for those men and women who have little or no background in science. Thus, I have attempted to address pertinent issues as simply as possible --- fully recognizing that those who have studied intensively in specialized areas of science may accuse this book of being too simplistic.

The book touches on the evolution of a creationist (me) but **emphasizes** the **inherent conflicts between evolutionary theory and the Bible**. This work is a compilation of thoughts and writings that God used to change my belief system.

It is my conviction that the Old and New Testaments of the Bible are God's inspired, infallible, inerrant Word. The Bible is to be interpreted in the normal, historical, grammatical, literal fashion. Yes, the Bible uses figures of speech, but they are evident when used. The King James Version of the Bible is quoted throughout because of its universal acceptance.

When I use the term "evolution" I am referring to the idea that after the earth was formed it took millions of years to produce organic molecules and then many more millions of years of evolutionary processes and "survival of the fittest" to produce people.   I refer to evolution as it encompasses the molecules to man theory.

For those of you who read with extreme concentration, never missing a word or a thought, please overlook the repetitions. Some of us need repetition so that we can better understand a concept.

Finally, when speaking about origins (Where did I come from?), we are dealing with a system of faith. It may be faith in eternal God or faith in eternal matter and energy. This book will attempt to help the reader discern which system of thought about our beginnings he or she believes. Is it the impersonal, plus chance, plus billions of years? Or is there an infinite Creator/Designer capable of creating the universe and all it contains in six 24 hour days?

I would encourage parents and young people to start building a personal library of good creationist literature. Helpful creationist books and organizations have been included here for your reference. Many high school and college students are writing reports from a creationist perspective and Professors can appreciate their excellently documented scholarship even when they disagree with the creationist's position.

My personal thanks to all of the courageous authors who have influenced me and suffered for the sake of righteousness in their endeavors to glorify our Lord through their writings. In 1971 the first book I read impacted me greatly. It was The Genesis Flood by Dr. Henry Morris and Dr. John Whitcomb. The second book was written by Dr. Bolton Davidheizer and is entitled Evolution and the

<u>Christian Faith</u>. These two books played a significant role in my evolution out of evolutionary thinking.

I know that apart from God's Spirit working within people's hearts to convict them of truth, mere human efforts to make an apologetic and change people's minds are futile. I also believe that the "Battle is the Lord's" (II Chronicles 20:15) & yet He somehow delights to use His saints in the battles - for His ultimate eternal glory. I humbly bow before my Creator and Savior, the Lord Jesus Christ, and am trusting Him to use His Word, which is quoted throughout this book, to speak to your heart. He is faithful (II Tim. 2:13) and His Word is true (John 17:17) and living and powerful and sharper than any two-edged sword (Hebrews 4:12). His truth will ultimately prevail -- eternally!

MARVELS OF GOD'S CREATION

At the end of each chapter a "Marvel of God's Creation" will be inserted to display the uniqueness of certain creatures in God's creation. Evolutionary belief is based on the premise that plants and animals don't evolve something new until it is needed. Evolution simply cannot explain the origin of these unique animals. There is no way their existence could have happened apart from special creation. They would have "died in process" trying to evolve the necessary equipment and functions to maintain life. Brilliant men have spent lifetimes attempting to prove creatures evolved. That job has yet to be accomplished!

AN ADMONITION

If you have time to read
this book today, but have not
taken the time to read your Bible,
then you do not have time
to read this book!

1

THE EVOLUTION OF A CREATIONIST

Frustration was not an adequate word to describe my feelings! Which was true -- evolution and billions of years, or creation in six 24-hour days? Two of my students at Baylor College of Dentistry had challenged me to investigate the possibility that the God of the Bible had created everything in six 24-hour days, as described in Genesis 1. My first reaction was, "Only an ignorant fool would believe in those ancient myths of the Book of Genesis."

I was an evolutionist. My years as a biology major at Bucknell University and a dental major at the University of Pittsburgh had convinced me that we are here because of evolutionary processes -- all very logical and explainable through the Scientific Method. This was A.D. 1971! We were living in the days of modern, hi-tech-science which had "proven" evolution to be true. And yet, these two dental students were brilliant young men.   They held advanced degrees in the sciences. Surely, there must be a simple way to prove that their six-day view of creation was wrong. One of the questions those two dental students asked me was this: "Doctor Martin, have you ever heard of the concept of God creating things with the appearance of age?" At that point in my pilgrimage, I certainly had not, but it sparked a desire to learn more. And thus the frustration began.

FLASHBACK

The seed of my frustration was planted in September of 1966.   I was attending USAF Basic Medical Training at Wichita Falls, Texas. It was the height of the Viet Nam War, and I had been given orders to report in at Andrews Air Force Base in Washington, D.C., upon completion of Basic Training. I was to be one of five dentists to serve the pilots and crews of President Johnson's presidential fleet -- the 89th Military Airlift Wing.

The seed was a brief prayer. As I sat at the Officer's Club that September night, I decided to clear things up with the God of the Bible (if He was really there). If He could part the Red Sea, turn water into wine, and raise the dead, He could answer a simple prayer. This was my prayer: "God, if you are up there, you have two choices. Either you can show me the girl I am going to marry, or you will see the wildest Air Force officer you have ever seen." I instantly thought, "Whew, nobody heard that prayer, I'm going out and live it up!"

Except God did hear that prayer. I met my wife-to-be that very day! We had a date the next night, and I told Jenna Dee that I was going to marry her.   I knew I would. The God of the Bible had answered my specific prayer on the day that I uttered it to Him.

Upon my arrival to Washington, D.C., I decided to go to church and learn more about God. As I left church that first Sunday, the pastor shook my hand and asked if there was anything he could do to help me spiritually. I told him that anything he could do would help me spiritually, because at that point I was a big zero. Pastor Charlie Warford asked me to get up on Monday mornings at 6:00 a.m. and read the Bible with him. I used to like to argue with people about the Bible, but I'd never really read it. So we read Matthew, Mark, and Luke, and we were in John, chapter 3, verse 16, when God got my attention. This verse said, **"For God so loved the world, that He gave His only begotten Son, that whosoever believeth in him should not perish, but have everlasting life."** It was the first phrase that got my attention. I was part of the world, had a heavy commitment to the world, and I knew it. That verse said to my heart that God loved me! I got on my knees with Pastor Warford and committed my life to the Lord Jesus Christ. The seed had been planted and was beginning to sprout.

At the point in time I came to faith in Jesus Christ as my Savior, my sins were all forgiven, and I was given everlasting life. But something else happened which I was only later to realize. I had gone from being an "agnostic evolutionist" to being a "theistic evolutionist". That meant that now I believed in God <u>and</u> that He used evolution over billions of years to create the universe and everything in it. I honestly believed that evolution was the only scientifically accurate option for how we got here. It was the "Big Bang", plus time, plus chance. Or, in other words, "nothing plus no one equals everything".

EVERYONE BELIEVES BY FAITH

My university science professors had not told me that I was making some significant assumptions by believing in the Big Bang model. The "Big Bang" is the belief that the universe and all it contains is the result of matter, so dense that the matter was invisible, suddenly exploding in a mega-explosion labelled by evolutionary scientists as the "Big Bang". Many scientists believe that this explosion occurred between eight and twenty billion years ago. To accept the Big Bang, one must assume the existence of matter and energy to be eternal. The Big Bang model only attempts to explain the ordering of matter and energy, not their origin. Matter had to be eternally present before the Big Bang or there would have been nothing there to go "Boom!". We discover here that everyone on earth believes in something <u>eternal</u> by faith. It is either faith in eternal matter and energy <u>or</u> faith in eternal God.

Why is this belief by faith? Because it is beyond the reach of science to test. There are no experiments that can test who or what was here when the universe began. Consequently, when we speak of origins, neither the creation model nor the evolution model can be tested or verified by reproducible scientific experiments. This takes both models of origins out of the realm of science and into the arena of <u>faith</u>.

God in His infinite genius has designed His creation so that, no matter which view of origins you believe, you are face to face with God. If matter and energy were eternal, they would be - by the time of the Big Bang - in a state of equilibrium. That means everything would be equal and non-reactive. A car is like that. The car sits there in neutral and doesn't do anything until it is turned on. Starting the engine explodes the gasoline which gives the power to move the car.

Science tells us that when matter is somewhere for a long enough time (eternity past), it will eventually stop doing anything and just sit there in neutral like a car. This is a part of the second law of Thermodynamics and is called Zeroeth Entropy. Before the Big Bang, all matter and energy, if eternal, would be in neutral. It's like the car when it is turned off and in park on a flat driveway. It will not move until someone starts it up.

So, if everything was in neutral before the Big Bang, what made the Big Bang go "Boom!"? If you believe in the Big Bang and eternal matter and energy, you believe by faith that an outside "force" acted on this matter-in-neutral to supply the energy necessary to explode it into action. In reality, you are face to face with God. **"In the beginning, God!"**. The first question then is this: "Do I believe by faith in eternal matter and energy (which gives me the problem of how did the Big Bang go "Boom!"?); or do I believe by faith in eternal God? Everyone believes by faith in something eternal.

Philip E. Johnson, a First Amendment attorney who teaches law at the University of California, Berkeley, believes that the media all too often presents creationists as if they do not use or understand science. Johnson writes:

> "In fact, there is a great deal more to the creation - evolution controversy than meets the eye, or rather than meets the carefully cultivated media stereotype of "creationists" as Bible-quoting know-nothings who refuse to face up to the scientific evidence. The creationists may be wrong about many things, but they have at least one very important point to argue, a point that has been thoroughly obscured by all the attention paid to Noah's flood and other side issues. What science educators propose to teach as "evolution", and label as fact, is based not upon any incontrovertible empirical evidence *(scientifically proven facts, ed.)*,but upon a highly controversial philosophical presupposition. The controversy over evolution is therefore not going to go away as people become better educated on the subject. On the contrary,

the more people learn about the philosophical content of what scientists are calling the "fact of evolution," the less they are going to like it." [1]

Like many of us, Johnson is concerned that public school science teachers and university professors have moved out of the realm of "science" and into the sphere of religious teaching (faith) when they address the evolution of molecules to man as if it were scientific fact. In my years as a science major at Bucknell University and the University of Pittsburgh, I was taught that science and fossils prove evolution to be true -- that the important transitional steps in the evolution of one creature into another "occurred within its gaps". I now agree with Johnson when he questions current evolutionary theory and its adherents. The evolutionary model's "...mechanism accomplishes wonders of creativity not because the wonders can be demonstrated, but because they (evolutionists) cannot think of a more plausible explanation for the existence of wonders that does not involve an unacceptable creator, i.e., a being or force outside the world of Nature." [2] The political correctness of the day in which we live also dictates the abhorrence of any credibility or reality to a literal God who is, in fact, greater than science, because He is the Creator of all.

---

[1] Phillip E. Johnson, Evolution as Dogma: The Establishment of Naturalism (Dallas, TX: Haughton Publishing Company, 1990),pp. 1,2.

[2] Ibid., p. 7

GOD, THE CREATOR

Though the idea of Creator God outside the world of nature is unacceptable to the majority of evolutionists, the Bible teaches that eternal God created the universe and He did so *by* and *through* and *for* His only eternal Son, the Lord Jesus Christ. The eternal Son was there in the beginning of creation as can be seen in the plural pronouns of Genesis 1:26, **"Let *us* make man in *our* image, according to *our* likeness**." That He, the Son, was instrumental in the creation of all things is taught in the Gospel of John:

> **"In the beginning was the Word and the Word was with God and the Word was God. The same was in the beginning with God. All things were made by him; and without him was not any thing made that was made. In him was life; and the life was the light of men." (John 1:1-4)**

These verses of John verify that Jesus is the Creator, and that all things were made by Him. The book of Hebrews is another testimony that Jesus is the Creator of the world: **"God..., Hath in these last days spoken to us by *his* Son, whom he hath appointed heir of all things, by whom also he made the worlds;..."** (Hebrews 1:1-2). The letter to the Colossians also refers to the Lord Jesus as the Creator of all things, and it goes on to name Him as the One Who **"holds all things together"** (Colossians 1:15-17).

Scientists say, "We have a problem. There are not enough stars and moons and asteroids to hold the universe together". This is called the "Missing Mass" problem. Everything should be flying apart, but it is staying together. A creationist can say, "I know what holds the universe together in spite of the 'Missing Mass' problem. The Lord Jesus, the Creator holds it all together by His great power (Hebrews 1 and Colossians 1)." When the Bible refers to science, it may not be exhaustive, but it is accurate. We can trust it.

The Scriptures tell us that the world came into being, not as a result of cosmic chance, but as a special creation with a unique purpose. God desired someone who would bring glory to Himself and with whom He could have fellowship. Ultimately, the Creator would step into time and His creation to become the Savior. But more about that later.

In the ancient Hebrew of the Old Testament a word is repeated to emphasize it. For example, Isaiah 6:3 uses repetition to tell us that God is infinitely holy: **"*Holy, Holy, Holy* is the Lord of hosts, the whole earth is full of His glory."** You cannot get any holier than God. The Hebrew language uses the same word three times to show the total absolute holiness of God. In a similar way, Genesis emphasizes the fact of creation. Moses, under the inspiration of the Holy Spirit, writes:

> **"This is the book of the generations of Adam. In the day that God <u>created</u> man, in the likeness of God made he him; Male and female <u>created</u> he them; and blessed them, and called their name Adam, in the day when they were <u>created</u>."**
> **(Genesis 5:1-2 emphasis added)**

MAN, THE CREATED

Man was created, created, created! You cannot get any more emphatic than that. The Bible does not say man evolved, evolved, evolved. If God wanted to indicate that man had come about through ages of evolutionary changes, He surely could have. But His Word is Truth and the Truth says man was <u>created</u>.

Not only was man created by the Lord Jesus, but he was created in God's own image. Did God, who "spoke the creation into existence", have to use millions of years of evolutionary mistakes to finally achieve His own image in man? Of course not!

If people really did evolve from monkey-like creatures, then the question arises, "What about the Virgin Mary? Was Mary, the human mother of the Lord Jesus, composed of made-over monkey genes?" If Mary was a highly evolved, distant relative of monkeys, then is our Lord also genetically related to the primates? Mary was created in the image of God, not in the lineage of monkeys.

The Bible tells us that God created man in His own image as an instant creation (Genesis 1:27). Jesus, the Creator, verifies this in Mark 10:6. He states: **"But from the beginning of the creation, God made them male and female."** The context of Mark 10:6 is divorce. We all know that cockroaches, rabbits and rats do not get divorces. The creator is talking about people. People get divorces. The Creator of one-man/one-woman-'til-death-do-us-part marriage tells us that divorce is not His solution to problems of pride and selfishness in marriage. (If you would like to read some of what the Bible says about this please refer to Malachi 2:13-16; Deuteronomy 24:1-5; Matthew 5:31,32; Matthew 19:3-12; Mark 10:1-12; Luke 16:18; I Corinthians 7:10-16). People, created instantly in God's image, were there in the beginning. [3]

If we believe what the Bible says (and this book will argue that there is no "scientific" proof not to), Mark 10:6 alone destroys all evolutionary teaching. There were male and female people on earth from the beginning. The Creator says so. That leaves no room at all for billions of years of transitional animal forms (missing links) gradually evolving from a single cell through monkey-like creatures to man.

---

[3] I heard this argument first on a tape dealing with the evolution/creation controversy by Floyd Jones Ministries, 8222 Glencliffe Lane, Houston, Tx 77070.

MAN CREATED FULLY MATURE

If it is true that there were people here as male and female people from the very beginning, then God created them as instant adults. He created Adam, a full-grown (totally mature) adult who was only one second old. From Adam's rib (taken during the first general anesthetic!), God created instantly the first woman, Eve, complete and mature.

Adam woke up and did not see a baby girl. He was introduced to Eve, his fully grown wife.

If Adam had asked, "Eve, how old are you?" she would have answered, "One minute old, Adam." She was created with the appearance of age. She looked perhaps 25 years old, but she had to wait a whole year to celebrate her first birthday. If Eve said, "Adam, I'm hungry," he could have reached out and picked a ripe peach, though its tree was only three days old. God also created fully mature trees. They looked old, and bore ripe fruit, but they were only three days old. These three-day-old trees were growing in soil that was created fully developed. In this soil, ferns were thriving and flowers blooming. Huge, minutes to hours-old dinosaurs were walking the earth with Adam and Eve (fortunately they ate plants and not people, Genesis 1:30). Even the light beams from the stars could have been created at the instant God created the stars. It might appear to scientists that light from the farthest stars took millions of years to get to earth, but if God created fully mature systems then that light beam may only be as old as the star itself. (See Chapter 10, **Light From The Farthest Stars**, for further discussion of this subject.)

When I am addressing the issue of creation with maturity (or the appearance of age) with a class of college students, invariably a hand will go up at that point of the discussion.

The student will say, "Then God is a liar. He created something that is not what it appears to be if He created Adam, Eve, and dinosaurs full grown. They looked old, but were not old." No, God is not a liar. He told us exactly what He did in Genesis 1 and 2. Our problem is that we do not think we can believe it. Instead of believing the Bible, we have accepted the speculative theories of evolution.

Remember that in Hebrews 1, Colossians 1 and John 1, God tells us that Jesus is the Creator. Is it outside of the ability of God to create with the appearance of age? The Creator stepped into space-time-history as the Savior. He performed His first miracle during the wedding feast at Cana as recorded in John 2.

JESUS CREATED AGED WINE

Decades before Jesus and the Apostle John walked the streets of Cana, the Hebrew Old Testament was translated into Greek. This translation is called the LXX or the Septuagint. As John wrote the first two chapters of his gospel, he seemingly had in mind the first two chapters of the Septuagint Old Testament. Not only is the use of the Greek language similar, but John 1 and Genesis 1 talk about the beginning of the world and John 2 and Genesis 2 deal with a man and a woman moving into marriage.

As recorded in John 2 the marriage party at Cana had run out of wine. There were six stone waterpots full of water, which Jesus turned into wine. The servants took some of this new wine to the headwaiter. After tasting it he said, **"Every man at the beginning doth set forth good wine; and when men have well drunk, then that which is worse; but thou hast kept the good wine until now." (John 2:10)**

How is good wine produced? It must be aged. How old was this wine? Only a minute or two. The Creator steps into time and performs His first miracle to **"manifest forth His glory". (John 2:11).** He wants His disciples to make no mistake as to who He is. In doing so, He creates something (wine) with the appearance of age. The seconds-old wine tasted like aged wine. How many water pots does the Biblical account of John record? Six! How many days did God work in the creation week? Six! As John writes his Gospel he could be thinking about Genesis 1 and 2. In Genesis, God created the universe with the appearance of age in six days. In John 2, God created wine with the appearance of age in six water pots.

Scripture has one interpretation; however, it can have many applications. One of the applications of John 2 is that the Creator does not need time. He can create whatever He wants to create and make it appear to "have some years" on it. Creations that are new can appear to have gone through a process that required time -- but there was no time. Jesus manifested His glory as He performed His earthly miracles, without the use of time, just as He had created each aspect of the universe, instantly complete and fully functional.

PETER AIMS TO KILL

When Judas Iscariot came with a mob to betray Jesus, Peter grabbed a sword and aimed it at the head of one of them. The person ducked, and Peter succeeded in cutting off only the mobster's ear. Did Jesus pick up the ear, get out His suture kit, sew the ear back on and say, "Come back in two weeks and we'll take out your stitches?" Of course not! He put the ear back on the person -- no stitches, no healing process, no time involved. You see, the God of the Bible does not need time. There is no way to reattach an ear without the process of days of healing... unless you are God.

Our Creator does not need time to do what we humans (limited and finite) would dogmatically say requires time!

GOD CREATED TIME

God created time. He is not subject to it, since He is eternal and time is temporary. That is the message of II Peter 3:8, **"But, beloved, be not ignorant of this one thing, that one day is with the Lord as a thousand years, and a thousand years as one day."** II Peter 3:8 does not teach that each day of the creation week was 1,000 years or a longer period of time or vice versa (1,000 years as a day), but rather it shows that God is above time. The context of II Peter 3:8,9 is that time means nothing to God as He waits for us to come to repentance!

All of the miracles of our Creator, with the exception, perhaps, of walking on water, appear to have needed time! Our Lord did not need time for His miracles, and He did not need time to create the universe. For us to believe that God created the universe in a literal six-day, 24-hour/day week (as recorded in Genesis), we must assume that He can and will create things with the appearance of age. <u>His miracles tell us that this is consistent with His power and His character</u>. We can believe the Bible in the normal historical and grammatical sense of its meaning. As we will see in the chapters ahead, there is no scientific reason not to believe the Holy Scriptures as they are written. Of course, I did not know these things back in 1971, and twenty-three years later I am still learning. As I talked with those Baylor students, I began to realize that evolutionary theory and the Biblical creation account cannot be merged. Even the belief that God used evolutionary processes over extended periods of time to change primitive molecules into you and me (Theistic Evolution) is inadequate. It portrays a vicious, stupid God who needed millions of years (of ferocious animals eating animals or "survival of the fittest"), to produce something He considered perfect enough to announce that man was finally in His own image. Evolution destroys God, His infinite power and His image. Furthermore, evolution enslaves God to the restrictive boundaries of time.

Could it be that molecules-to-man evolution is not based on true science, but upon many unprovable assumptions? We will consider this in Chapter Two.

MARVEL OF GOD'S CREATION #1
The Bombardier Beetle

If there is any creature on earth that could not possibly have evolved, that creature is the Bombardier Beetle. It needed God to create it with all its systems fully functional.

> "...the bombardier (beetle) does appear to be unique in the animal kingdom. Its defense system is extraordinarily intricate, a cross between tear gas and a tommy gun. When the beetle senses danger, it internally mixes enzymes contained in one body chamber with concentrated solutions of some rather harmless compounds, hydrogen peroxide and hydroquinones, confined to a second chamber. This generates a noxious spray of caustic benzoquinones, which explodes from its body at a boiling 212° F.
> What is more, the fluid is pumped through twin rear nozzles, which can be rotated, like a B-17's gun turret, to hit a hungry ant or frog with bull's eye accuracy." [4] -Time Magazine

Evolutionary theory has big problems when attempting to explain the existence and complexity of the Bombardier. Each stage in the evolution of its special chemicals would have led to its destruction.

This one-half inch insect mixes chemicals which violently react to produce something similar to an explosion. How could the bombardier beetle have evolved this means of defense without killing itself in the process? This problem has the members of the evolutionary establishment scratching their heads. Evolutionary theory says that you do

---

[4] Natalie Angier reported by Rick Thompson/San Francisco, *Time Magazine* (February 25, 1985), p. 70

not evolve something until you know you need it. In other words a new enzyme or chemical or organ or fin or beak or bone will not evolve until the creature realizes it needs the new improvement. The bombardier beetle would not have known it needed a mechanism to prevent these chemicals from blowing it up until it mixed the chemicals and blew itself up. Naturally, it could not evolve after it was dead, so how did it get here? The evolutionists say, "We don't know".

To prevent its own destruction the little bug manufactures another chemical, called an inhibitor, and mixes it in with the explosive chemicals. But with the inhibitor, it would not be able to use the explosion of hot, burning liquid and gases to discourage its enemies. A spider would eat it because the beetle has no solution to explode to protect itself. Again, we have a dead beetle. Dead bugs cannot evolve the next chemical needed to release the protective reaction. That chemical turns out to be an anti-inhibitor. When the anti-inhibitor is added to the other chemicals, an explosive reaction does occur and the beetle is able to defend itself. There is still another problem, however: the beetle must have an especially tough "combustion chamber" and that chamber must have an outlet for the violent reaction to release its energy, or once again we have a dead bug. Problem solved: this unique creature has the necessary equipment, including twin-tail tubes to "exhaust" its defensive reaction. These tubes can be aimed at enemies in a 180° arc from straight to the rear, to directly toward the front. Amazingly, it does not shoot friendly creatures but only its enemies! How does a one-half inch long insect know how to aim at and shoot only enemies? And, how did its incredibly complex nervous system and advanced chemical system evolve? There is nothing like the Bombardier beetle in the entire animal kingdom.

Is this an example of the "impersonal, plus time, plus chance" or is it an example of a special, intricate creation by a God who is intimately involved with His creatures? Which system of belief can best explain the marvelous Bombardier Beetle: Evolution or Creation? [5]

---

[5] Duane Gish, Ph.D., *Dinosaurs Those Terrible Lizards* (San Diego: Creation Life Publishers), pp. 50-55. These pages describe the Bombardier Beetle. This children's book is primarily about dinosaurs.

2

....AND THEN CAME ASSUMPTIONS

Many college science professors never tell their students that the evolutionary model of one cell to man is based on assumptions. What is an assumption? It is something taken for granted and supposed to be true.[6] As a six-day creationist, I believe God created the universe and everything in it fully mature (with the appearance of age). I cannot prove this with scientific experiments so this belief is called an assumption. I suppose it to be true. Evolutionists likewise have assumptions. They take many necessary steps for granted in the molecules-to-man model. In other words,

---

[6] *Webster's Third New International Dictionary*, p. 133, G. & C. Meriam Company, Publishers, Springfield, Mass., U.S.A., 1981.

24

evolutionists assume that non-living chemicals gave rise to that first living cell which, in turn, evolved into ever and ever more complex forms of life. <u>There are no scientific experiments to prove the molecules-to-man scenario.</u>

Writing as an evolutionist, G. A. Kerkut lists the major assumptions of evolution. These are the basic theories an evolutionist "takes for granted" or "<u>supposes</u>" to be true. All of the "molecules-to-man science" is built upon these assumptions, but you rarely, if ever, see them listed in a high school or college textbook.

"There are seven basic assumptions that are often not mentioned during discussions of evolution. Many evolutionists ignore the first six assumptions and only consider the seventh. The assumptions are as follows:

1.   The first assumption is that non-living things gave rise to living material, i.e., spontaneous generation occurred.

2.   The second assumption is that spontaneous generation occurred only once.

3.   The third assumption is that viruses, bacteria, plants and animals are all related.

4.   The fourth assumption is that protozoa (single-celled life forms) gave rise to metazoa (multiple-celled life forms).

5.   The fifth assumption is that various invertebrate phyla are interrelated.

6.   The sixth assumption is that the invertebrates gave rise to the vertebrates.

7.   The seventh assumption is that within the vertebrates the fish gave rise to amphibia, the amphibia to reptiles and the reptiles to birds and mammals." [7]

---

[7] G. A. Kerkut, *Implications of Evolution* (New York: Pergamon Press, 1960), chapter 2 p. 6.

MOLECULES-TO-MAN IS ASSUMED

What Dr. Kerkut has listed as "assumptions" is the whole of evolutionary teaching. In other words, there is no <u>factual</u> (experimentally testable and reproducible) science which supports evolution. The process of moving from non-living things to the first living, reproducing cell to man and giant Redwood trees <u>is all an assumption</u>.

Dr. Kerkut clearly states the evolutionary assumption that all life is related to that first cell. However, through the use of phase-electron microscopes scientists have discovered that there are consistent differences in cellular substance in various kinds of animals. When studied microscopically, the living things of the evolutionary tree do not appear to be related to each other at all. I Corinthians 15:39 records: **"All flesh is not the same flesh: but there is one kind of flesh of men, another flesh of beasts, another flesh of fishes, and another of birds."** This was written 1900 years before scientists "discovered" the differences in the basic cellular components of the various kinds of living creatures. God created life and inspired His apostles and prophets to record details of His creation, which scientists are just beginning to discover. God says there are different types of flesh in the bodies of His earthly creatures. But there are also different types of heavenly bodies -- the stars are different from each other and not the same as the moon (I Cor. 15:41). Astronomers estimate there may be one trillion-trillion stars. The best English dictionaries have less than 800,000 words. Yet, the God of the Bible has a name and a number for each star, **"...He calleth them all by names..."**! (Isaiah 40:26) God is infinite in His power and wisdom.

From the biggest star to the smallest atom, the magnitude and complexity of the universe is unexplainable, except in terms of a creative designer who is infinitely above any "chance processes" or human technology.

Many scientists assume life came from non-living chemicals[8] and that this only happened once. They say that everything we see alive, whether plant or animal, came from that first, primordial, single cell. Most evolutionists do not believe that one kind of life began in the Amazon and another in Africa and another in Arizona. They believe non-life gave birth to life in one cell that became the ancestor of the entire plant and animal kingdoms.

Why do scientists such as Dr. Kerkut assume this startling event happened only once? Because the chances of life evolving from non-life are so astronomically high as to be impossible without an intelligent designer. Dr. Henry Morris and Dr. Gary Parker of the Institute for Creation Research have recorded the probability of the chance origin of life in their revised book, <u>What is Creation Science?</u> (pp. 269-276). If all the universe was crammed with electron particles, the maximum number of particles would be ten to the power of 130. If each particle could do one hundred billion-billion events (steps in ever onward and upward evolution) every second for 3,000 billion years (100 times older than anyone says the universe is), then in the span of history of the universe 10 to the one-hundred seventieth power events could possibly happen. But to get a series of even 1,500 events to happen in order [and without God's help] (events that might be moving from non-living chemicals to a living cell), there is only one chance in ten to the power of 450! This means that the probability of evolution even getting started is zero. There aren't enough

---

[8] <u>The Mystery of Life's Origin</u> presents the scientific position that chemical evolution is impossible. This book by Doctors of Chemistry has not been answered by the evolutionists. Non-living chemicals will not ultimately generate reproducing life. The chemistry does not work that way. Charles Thaxton, Walter Bradley, Roger Olsen, *The Mystery of Life's Origin: Reassessing Current Theories* (N.Y.: Philosophical Library, Inc., 1984).

electrons in the universe to, by chance, generate a single living cell of a single evolutionary scientist. And yet, these scientists who do not believe in God are here. How did they get here? Without belief in God, the only option these people have is the evolution of non-living chemicals over aeons of time into a living cell and ultimately into man.

For nearly 150 years some of the most brilliant scientists in the world have attempted to convert non-living chemicals into some form of reproducible life. No one has done it.

A CELL IS NOT SIMPLE

A single reproducible cell is far from simple. Dr. Leon Long, of the Department of Geological Sciences at the University of Texas at Austin, writes as an evolutionist:

> "Among the first organisms were the lowly bacteria and blue-green algae. They are about as simple as a self-sufficient cell can be, which is none too simple, considering that a bacterium can synthesize some 3,000 to 6,000 compounds at a rate of about 1 million reactions per second! Cells of bacteria and blue-green algae contain just a single molecule of DNA, and they lack well-defined internal structures, such as a nucleus, chromosomes, and internal membranes." [9]

Is it any wonder scientists claim that life from non-living chemicals only happened once? According to Dr. Long, the simplest forms of life can perform one million reactions per second! Something that complex obviously needs a designer, a Creator.

---

[9] Leon E. Long, *Geology* (New York: McGraw-Hill Book Company, 1974), p. 172.

Scientists do not talk very much about the evolution of the cell membrane. The membrane that provides the outside wall (or skin) of the cell is highly complex. This membrane permits specific concentrations of certain chemicals and solutions into and out of the cell. If the concentrations of some of these chemicals vary by even 1/100%, the cell will die. At a microscopic spot in the universe, how did those chemicals all get together in the correct configurations and concentrations and at the same instant? In addition, how did the cell membrane form around them at just the right moment permitting only specific concentrations of chemicals in and out of the cell ("knowing", of course, what those chemicals must and must not be)? And how could all of this somehow know how to reproduce itself and not die in the process?

The God of the Bible said He *created, created, created*! His creation defies the speculations of the evolutionist. Creation necessitates a designer. It demands fully functional life from the beginning. Biology acknowledges this with its most well-proven law, the law of Biogenesis: Life generates life. If something is alive, it is alive because something else alive produced it. The Bible tells us the living God is the Creator of life, and that statement agrees with what we see in biology. Life always comes from life.

And yet, evolutionary chemists construct laboratory experiments that attempt to display the means by which life began without God. Many of these experimenters believe that the atmosphere of primitive Earth was quite different than it is today. The atmosphere of the planet Jupiter is thought to resemble that of early Earth. Water vapor, hydrogen, ammonia and methane were the supposed ingredients. In 1953, a chemist, Dr. Stanley Miller, placed these four ingredients into a glass jar which he heated and into which he sent sparks of electricity. He noticed a pink fluid coming off into his trap. This fluid contained some amino acids. Amino acids are the building blocks of proteins. Proteins are very much a part of living tissue, but they are not life. The Miller-type experiments do not display chemicals marching ever onward and upward until reproducing life is generated, yet evolution in this manner is assumed to have happened. As a matter of fact, there is no evidence in the rocks of Earth or the present oceans that water vapor, hydrogen, ammonia and methane ever existed in the concentrations necessary for Miller's experiments to accurately occur in nature.

The claim that chemical evolution is impossible, as presented in <u>The Mystery of Life's Origin</u> [8], has yet to be refuted. Random chemical reactions do not produce life! Dr. Stanley Miller and his followers did not produce anything with raw chemicals that even approaches life. Dennis Petersen in his informative book, <u>Unlocking the Mysteries of Creation</u>, quotes Dr. Henry Morris who says it this way:

> "Unknown chemicals in the primordial past...through...
>   Unknown processes which no longer exist...produced...
>   Unknown life forms which are not to be found...but could through...
>   Unknown reproduction methods spawn new life...in an...
>   Unknown atmospheric composition..in an...
>   Unknown oceanic soup complex...at an...
>   Unknown time and place."

Prove any of these unknowns of evolution with experimentally testable science and the Nobel Science prize will be yours!

A PERSONAL DESIGNER CREATES LIFE

Let us not forget--the evolutionist says there was no God, no higher power, no designer, no person behind the beginning of life.

It was the impersonal (no person), plus time, plus chance (or, no one plus nothing equals everything!) So, even if the Stanley Miller experiments did prove chemical evolution is possible, <u>which they did not do</u>, you still have a personal designer (Miller) making his creation. Does a personal designer-scientist, doing experiments in a carefully controlled laboratory, prove that the creation of life occurred without any creator designer (no God) in a totally random-chance primordial ooze? Of course not. Our God is worthy to receive the honor and the glory and the praise because He created all things (Rev. 4:11). We can trust God and His Word, the Bible. Nothing is too difficult for Him (Jeremiah 32:17).....He is the God of the impossible (Luke 1:37).

HAS ANYONE SEEN AN ELECTRON?

One of the greatest scientists of the space age, Dr. Werner von Braun stated:

"One cannot be exposed to the law and order of the universe without concluding that there must be design and purpose behind it all...The better we understand the intricacies of the universe and all it harbors, the more reason we have found to marvel at the inherent design upon which it is based...

To be forced to believe only one conclusion -- that everything in the universe happened by chance -- would violate the very objectivity of science itself...What random process could produce the brains of man or the system of the human eye? They (evolutionists) challenge science to prove the existence of God. But must we really light a candle to see the sun?...they say they cannot visualize a designer. Well, can a physicist visualize an electron?...What strange rationale makes some physicists accept the inconceivable electron as real while refusing to accept the reality of a Designer on the ground that they cannot conceive Him?..." [10]

Ask any scientist if he believes in electrons. He will answer, "Certainly". Ask that same scientist if he or she has ever seen an electron, and they will say, "No". Scientists believe in electrons by faith as they observe the results of electron activity.

Is this not similar to faith in God? We do not see God, but we do "see" Him through His handiwork, the creation. Romans 1 explains that as we study the intricacies of the macro- and micro-universes, we should think about who designed them, who makes them work, and who holds them together.

FOOLISH SPECULATIONS

When scientists examine the largest stars and the smallest atoms and do not honor God as their Creator and give thanks to Him, they are reduced to foolish speculations (Romans 1:18-23). Could the evolution of man from a single cell be a foolish speculation? Dr. Harrison Matthews, the writer of the introduction to Darwin's <u>Origin of Species by Means of Natural Selection or the Preservation of Favoured Races in the Struggle for Life</u>, states:

"The fact of evolution is the backbone of biology, and biology is thus in the peculiar position of being a science founded on an unproved theory -- is it then a science or a faith? Belief in the theory of evolution is thus exactly parallel to belief in special

---

[10] Dennis R. Petersen, *Unlocking the Mysteries of Creation*, Vol. 1 (El Cajon: Master Books, 1988), p. 63, as quoted from the <u>Bible Science Newsletter</u>, May, 1974, p.8

creation -- both are concepts which believers know to be true, but neither, up to the present, has been capable of proof." [11]

Dr. Matthews, an evolutionist, says evolution has no scientific proof. It is a speculation of faith. Yet, Dr. Ernst Mayr, professor emeritus of Harvard University, writes:

> "Since Darwin, every <u>knowing</u> person agrees man descended from the apes. Today, there is no such thing as the theory of evolution. It is the fact of evolution." [12]

<u>Omni Magazine</u> promotes evolution. Dr. Mayr presents godless evolution as fact, even though the Creator says in Romans 1 that all men know better: **"For the wrath of God is revealed from heaven against all ungodliness and unrighteousness of men, who hold (suppress) the truth in unrighteousness; because that which may be known of God is manifest in them; for God hath shewed it unto them (Romans 1:18-19)."** Romans 1:22 adds: **"Professing themselves to be wise, they became fools."**

Dr. T.N. Tahmisian of the Atomic Energy Commission agrees:

> "Scientists who go about teaching that evolution is a fact of life are great con-men, and the story they are telling may be the greatest hoax ever. In explaining evolution, we do not have one iota of fact." [13]

---

[11] L. Harrison Matthews, FRS, "Introduction," Charles Darwin, *Origin of Species by Means of Natural Selection or the Preservation of Favoured Races in the Struggle for Life* (London: J.M. Dent and Sons, 1971), p. xi, as quoted in *The Revised Quote Book*, ed. Andrew Snelling, Ph.D. (Institute for Creation Research, P.O. Box 2667, El Cajon, Calif. 92021), p. 2. For many more quotes that negate evolution from the literature of the evolutionary scientists, purchase *The Quote Book*. The cost is around $4.00 and well worth it.

[12] Dr. Ernst Mayr, *Omni Magazine*, February, 1983, p. 74.

[13] Dr. T. N. Tahmisian, "The Fresno Bee", August 20, 1959, as quoted in <u>The Revised Quote Book</u>, p. 5.

Isaac Asimov and Carl Sagan have presented evolution as no longer a theory, but a proven fact. They have done this without a single iota of fact. Evolutionist, D.M.S. Watson said it best:

> "Evolution itself is accepted by zoologists not because it has been observed to occur or is supported by logically coherent arguments, but because...no alternative explanation is credible.
> Whilst the fact of evolution is accepted by every biologist, the mode in which it has occurred and the mechanism by which it has been brought about are still disputable.
> ...the theory of evolution itself is a theory universally accepted not because it can be proved by logical coherent evidence to be true but because the only alternative is special creation, which is clearly incredible." [14]

The clearly incredible Creator says in Psalm 19:1:

"The heavens declare the glory of God; and the firmament sheweth His handiwork."

---

[14] D.M.S. Watson, "Adaptation," Nature, August 10, 1929, Vol. 124, #3119, pp. 231,233.

MARVEL OF GOD'S CREATION #2
The Incubator Bird

The Megapode or "incubator bird" of Australia is unique among birds. This three to four pound bird resembles a chicken or a small turkey. Some native Australians call it the brush turkey.

The incubator birds are unlike all other birds. So, if they evolved, from what did they evolve? Or what are they evolving into? A recent Scientific American article[15] offers precious little by way of an evolutionary explanation for the origins of this strange bird.

All birds use body heat to incubate their eggs except the incubator bird.

> "Instead, they pile up great heaps of debris which serve as incubators; the warmth of the fermenting compost does the work. In one species, the scrub fowl, a mound 20 feet high and 50 feet wide has been reported." [16]

Instead of using its own body heat to incubate its eggs (as does the chicken who sits on her eggs), the incubator bird uses fermentation heat or "...some use solar heat and others the heat produced by volcanic action." [17]

A bird that uses volcanic heat or the warmth of fermenting plant life to hatch its eggs: Incredible! If there

---

[15] Roger S. Seymour, "The Brush Turkey," *Scientific American*, Vol. 265, No. 6, December, 1991, pp. 108-114.

[16] Roger Tory Petersen, *Life Nature Library: The Birds* (New York: Time-Life Books, 1973), p. 140.

[17] *The New Encyclopedia Britannica*, Vol. 7 (Chicago: University of Chicago, 1990 edition), p. 1011.

are any creatures that could not possibly evolve, the Australian incubator bird joins the bombardier beetle as such a creature.

The female is responsible for two activities. First, she must test the nest to be sure it is adequate for incubating her eggs. What explanation can evolution offer for the ability of the hen to evaluate the suitability of a nest that may be dug three feet into the ground and extend 10 or more feet above ground and up to 50 feet across? And what would motivate a little three and one-half pound male bird to get busy constructing monstrous nest number two, should the hen reject his first effort?

After accepting the nest, the second responsibility of the female is performed. She lays 20 to 35 eggs at the rate of one egg every three days for up to seven months. "...As many as 16 eggs can exist in a normal mound at any one time." [18]   Each egg weighs about a half a pound and is as large as an ostrich egg. That is a tremendous amount of work for a three to four pound hen. No wonder that upon completion of her laying task, she leaves the nest, never to return. She takes no part in the incubation and raising of her chicks. This is not your normal evolutionary way!

At this point the male begins to perform his God-given job of managing the incubation of the deeply buried eggs. For incubator bird chicks to survive they demand a precise temperature of 91°F. Yes, exactly 91°F. If the male bird wants the chicks to survive, he will not let the temperature vary more then one degree on either side of 91°F! How does the daddy bird maintain a consistent temperature of 91°F in a mound of decaying plants and dirt?

Scientists differ on the mechanism they think the bird uses to measure the temperature. Some think the bird's thermometer is in its beak. Others believe the tongue can

---

[18] Ibid., Roger Seymour, p. 109.

distinguish 91°F and a few tenths of a percent above and below 91°F.

Here is the point: How could a bird evolve the ability to precisely measure temperatures with its beak or tongue? Evolution says nothing is evolved until it is needed. How would the incubator bird know it needed the ability to keep its eggs at 91°F? The chicks would get too hot or too cold and die before he figured it out. And dead creatures do not evolve into higher forms.

You may be asking, "Well, how does this bird keep those eggs at 91°F?" The male digs down into the nest and checks the temperature. On hot days, he may pile extra sand on top of the nest to shield it from the sun. He may even rearrange the entire pile of rotting leaves and grasses several times a day.

On cooler days, the male megapodes (which means big feet) will push material off the top of the nest to permit more sunlight to penetrate the decaying organic material. Or, to keep the humidity at 99.5% around the eggs, he may dig conical holes toward the eggs to get more moisture deeper into the nest. Keeping temperature and humidity just right is a big job. Concerning the precision needed for incubation temperature maintenance, Seymour writes:

> "This process is very precise: one centimeter of fresh material added to the mound can increase core temperature about 1½°C." [19]

Not only must the eggs be kept at 91°F and 99.5% humidity, but the chick must get enough air to breathe. The father provides the fresh air for the chicks as he daily digs down to the eggs. But the chick must get the air inside the

---

[19] Ibid., Roger Seymour, p. 110.

shell. The means to get air inside the shell was provided by the hen as she formed the shell. It has thousands of tiny holes (called pores) in it. These holes in the thick shell are shaped like conical ice cream cones with the narrowest part of the cone toward the chick. As the chick grows it cannot get enough air through the bottom of the cone so it begins to remove the inside layer of the shell. As it thins out the shell the holes get bigger (moving up the cone) and the chick can get more air. Amazing!

The way the chicks hatch is also unique among birds. Unlike other birds, they are ready to fly with full feathers as soon as they break out of the egg. Once they hatch, it takes up to three days for them to dig their way up out of the mound. How do they know they must dig their way out or else they die? They have not been instructed by either parent. Even so, they lie on their backs and dig up until they break out. <u>Clearly, the God of the Bible is involved with all aspects of His creation!</u>

Once the chicks dig out of the nest, they are on their own. They are not fed or cared for by either parent. When they are mature, the male will build a huge nest as an incubator for his mate's eggs. He will build this huge, precise mound without any instruction from his parents. This is not learned behavior.! How does the brush turkey know the importance of 91°F?

Credentialed men and women have the audacity to say that this bird is the product of the impersonal plus time plus chance. But truly, how could the incubator bird even exist? Only if the God of the Bible lives and is involved with His creatures.

3

HAS GOD BEEN TOPPLED?

One day my two creationist dental students asked me to give them a scientific explanation for how evolution occurs. In other words, they wanted me to defend my evolutionary beliefs by telling them the scientific evidence I could present as proof of how one creature evolves into another and whether that evidence conflicts with the Bible. Darwin seemed like the logical place to start searching for my answer. I believed the evidence was there somewhere, but I'd never been asked to prove it before. Did I ever get a shock! Darwin had no idea how one species of animal could evolve into another. He wrote to a friend in 1863:

> "When we descend to details we can prove that no one species has changed (i.e., we cannot prove that a single species has changed): nor can we prove that the supposed changes are beneficial, which is the groundwork of the theory. Nor can we

explain why some species have changed and others have not. The latter case seems to me hardly more difficult to understand precisely and in detail than the former case of supposed change." [20]

THE REALLY BIG QUESTION

Obviously, in 1863, four years after publishing <u>Origin of Species by Means of Natural Selection or the Preservation of Favoured Races in the Struggle for Life</u>, Darwin had no idea how one species might change into another. The only thing he thought he could prove was that "...no one species has changed." He could not even imagine what a "beneficial" change might look like. Scientists today remain as baffled as Darwin.

The world's leading evolutionary thinkers had a convention in Rome in 1981. They wanted to decide what makes one species evolve into another species, and how that change, from one animal or plant into another, might occur. Dr. Ernst Mayr, professor emeritus of Harvard, writes:

> "We had an international conference in Rome in 1981 on the mechanisms of speciation. It was attended by many of the leading botanists, zoologists, paleontologists, geneticists, cytologists and biologists. The one thing on which they all agreed was that we still have absolutely no idea what happens genetically during speciation. That's a damning statement, but it's the truth." [21]

These scientists in Rome in 1981 arrived at their conclusion, "We have no idea how evolution occurs"! Neither did Darwin in 1863! This, then, is the really big question of evolution: How does it happen? God says He

---

[20] <u>The Life and Letters of Charles Darwin</u>, Frances Darwin, Ed., N.Y.: Appleton & Co., 1898, Vol. 11, p. 210. (Darwin's letter to G. Benham, May 22, 1863).

[21] Dr. Ernst Mayr, *Omni Magazine*, February, 1983, p. 78.

created each thing **"after its kind"** (Genesis 1:11, 12, 21, 24, 25). Evolutionists say they do not know how "kinds" come into being. Which account do you believe? God's or the evolutionist's? My position is that God alone is worthy to be praised!

Scientists do not know how one species might change into another. They do not even know how a simple chemical compound might come about. Author and friend of evolution, Jeff Goldberg, records for us the thoughts of Hans Kosterlitz, one of the discoverers of the human body's natural pain killers, the enkephalins:

> "It is a question almost of God. Working on the enkephalins you get -- without being religious -- a commitment. You start to admire and wonder, how could that come about -- that plants and animals share such structurally similar chemicals? How, even after a million years of evolution, could the earth, with all its plants and creatures, be so very simple and unified?" [22]

Kosterlitz looked at the enkephalins, and his study of the micro-universe made him think about God. But he quickly adds the disclaimer "without being religious," as if thinking about God is not religious when studying only a small part of His creation. Apparently Kosterlitz believes God has nothing to do with science. Yet, when scientists look at the creation, God has intended for it to make them realize that there must be a Designer-God behind it all. However, most add their disclaimers and refuse to honor Him as God. God's Word (i.e. Romans 1:18-22) declares that their thinking is thereby reduced to foolish speculations (evolution over millions of years, etc.).

Kosterlitz questioned how plants and animals could "...share such structurally similar chemicals". If we examine

---

[22] Jeff Goldberg, *Anatomy of a Scientific Discovery* (N.Y.: Bantam Books, 1988), p. 211.

this sharing of chemicals from a creationist perspective, then God created life to fit in the common atmosphere of earth with a common food chain composed of certain basic chemicals. Similarities in creatures do not prove evolution, but more logically display the wisdom of God in creating plants and animals which, in all their diversity, can exist in a common environment. God designed all life to exist while using a few common basic chemicals in an atmosphere made mostly of oxygen and nitrogen. What genius the God of the Bible displays!

HAS GOD BEEN TOPPLED?

Jerry Adler, a science writer, reviews world class evolutionary thinker Stephen Jay Gould's book, <u>Wonderful Life</u>, with these words:

> "Science, having toppled God the Creator and exalted Man, now wants to raise E. coli and the rest of the seething mass of terrestrial life up there alongside him. This view does not deny the uniqueness of Homo sapiens and its distinctive contribution to life, human consciousness. It asserts, however, that there is nothing inherent in the laws of nature that directed evolution toward the production of human beings. There is nothing predestined about our current pre-eminence among large terrestrial fauna; we are the product of a whole series of contingent events in the history of our planet, any one of which could have been reversed to give rise to a different outcome.
>
> We are, in short, like every other creature that ever walked or slithered across the earth, an accident....
>
> The survivors...were lucky.

The story of life is one of periodic mass extinctions, which wiped out the majority of species on earth." [23]

Gould and Adler evidently believe that God has been "toppled", that science and man are exalted, and all of this is based on the "lucky survivors" of mass extinctions. So, evolution appears to be based upon death. Because of the death of the "unfit", the "fittest" survive. How might a scientist describe "unfit" life? Do evolutionists believe there is "unfit" life among us today? Did Hitler believe that? Hitler was an evolutionist and apparently thought he was speeding up the process of survival of the fittest. Evolution is not amoral. It is not neutral thinking. It promotes a value system that permits each individual to do what is right in his own eyes. Evolutionary thought encourages school curricular materials that force young minds to choose who is fit to survive, and who is unfit; who will be rescued in the lifeboat, and who will be left to die of exposure or drowning. No one but God is qualified to describe a certain life as fit or "unfit". Evolutionary thinking wrongly promotes man to the status of God. It forces people to make decisions (for instance about life and death, abortion, euthanasia, infanticide) that should remain with God alone.

WE SEE DEATH AND EXTINCTION, NOT EVOLUTION

Scientists are correct when they observe and publish the fact that mass extinctions have occurred in the past. In the present, extinctions are occurring on a daily basis. What science can prove with facts is that life is disappearing. Life of a wide variety of kinds of plants and animals is becoming

---

[23] Jerry Adler, *Newsweek*, November 20, 1989, p. 68.

extinct.   Does this prove that new life forms are now evolving or ever did evolve?   *Science has conclusively proven that life is dying and the universe is running down. The fossils are a record of death and extinction.   The "Cambrian Explosion"* [24] *is not an explosion of early life.   It is a fossil record of the death of millions of complex organisms that, for the most part, no longer exist.*   So, therefore, when we look at nature, we do not see emerging new life forms but rather death and extinction ... entropy in action.

The Creator-God of the Bible is the source of life (John 5:26ff). Jesus said,

> **"Verily, verily, I say unto you, He that heareth my word, and believeth on him that sent me, hath everlasting life,and shall not come into condemnation; but is passed from death unto life.**
>
> **Verily, verily, I say unto you, The hour is coming and now is, when the dead shall hear the voice of the Son of God: and they that hear shall live.**
>
> **For as the Father hath life in himself; so hath he given to the Son to have life in himself;**
>
> **And hath given him authority to execute judgment also, because he is the Son of man.**
>
> **Marvel not at this: for the hour is coming, in which all that are in the graves shall hear his voice,**
>
> **And shall come forth; they that have done good, unto the resurrection of life; and they that have done evil, unto the resurrection of damnation."   (John 5:24-29)**

---

[24] Geologists tell us that Cambrian rocks are the oldest rocks that contain numerous life-forms as fossils. Many of these rocks display extremely complex creatures that supposedly existed 600,000,000 years ago. Because there are so many types and numbers of fossil creatures they are referred to as the "Cambrian Explosion of Life". The Genesis flood is a scientifically feasible explanation for this massive and rapid destruction of living creatures. This universal flood occurred about 5,000 years ago, not 600,000,000!

God created life. Death came when the first man, Adam, and his wife, Eve, rebelled against their Creator and sinned. Romans 5:12 states:

> **"Wherefore, as by one man sin entered into the world, and death by sin; and so death passed upon all men, for that all have sinned:"**

I Corinthians 15:21 continues this teaching:

> **"For since by man came death, by man came also the resurrection of the dead."**

If death came as a result of the sin of Adam, then sin, decay and death were non-existent until the Fall. What is the fossil record? It is a testimony of death. Could we have millions of years of death and fossil "man" leading up to Adam when the Scriptures plainly teach "for by man (referring to Adam) came death?" Fossils are a record of death. Without death, there can be no fossils. Do we believe the Bible or do we believe the speculations of scientists? Scientists believe death began millions of years before man evolved onto the scene. The Bible records that death began with Adam.

THE BIBLE AND EVOLUTION IN CONFLICT

As God's creatures, we do not subject the Bible to science, we subject science to the Bible. The challenge whether to believe God and His Word or to believe science is presented by Scott Huse, a brilliant Christian thinker, in his excellent book, The Collapse of Evolution. The conflict of evolutionary theory against the Holy Scripture is impossible to reconcile. Huse lists 24 contrasts between the Bible and evolutionary thinking:

1. **Bible**: God is the Creator of all things (Genesis 1).
   Evolution: Natural chance processes can account for the existence of all things.

2. **Bible**: World created in six literal days (Genesis 1).
   Evolution: World evolved over aeons.

3. **Bible**: Creation is completed (Genesis 2:3).
   Evolution: Creative processes continuing.

4. **Bible**: Ocean before land (Genesis 1:2).
   Evolution: Land before oceans.

5. **Bible**: Atmosphere between two hydrospheres (Genesis 1:7).
   Evolution: Contiguous atmosphere and hydrosphere.

6. **Bible**: First life on land (Genesis 1:11).
   Evolution: Life began in the oceans.

7. **Bible**: First life was land plants (Genesis 1:11).
   Evolution: Marine organisms evolved first.

8. **Bible**: Earth before sun and stars (Genesis 1:14-19).
   Evolution: Sun and stars before earth.

9. **Bible**: Fruit trees before fishes (Genesis 1:11).
   Evolution: Fishes before fruit trees.

10. **Bible**: All stars made on the fourth day (Genesis 1:16).
    Evolution: Stars evolved at various times.

11. **Bible**: Birds and fishes created on the fifth day (Genesis 1:20, 21).
    Evolution: Fishes evolved hundreds of millions of years before birds appeared.

12. **Bible**: Birds before insects (Genesis 1:20, 21).
    Evolution: Insects before birds.

13. **Bible**: Whales before reptiles (Genesis 1:20-31).
Evolution: Reptiles before whales.

14. **Bible**: Birds before reptiles (Genesis 1:20-31).
Evolution: Reptiles before birds.

15. **Bible**: Man before rain (Genesis 2:5).
Evolution: Rain before man.

16. **Bible**: Man before woman (Genesis 2:21-22).
Evolution: Woman before man (by genetics).

17. **Bible**: Light before the sun (Genesis 1:3-19).
Evolution: Sun before any light.

18. **Bible**: Plants before the sun (Genesis 1:11-19).
Evolution: Sun before any plants.

19. **Bible**: Abundance and variety of marine life all at once (Genesis 1:20, 21).
Evolution: Marine life gradually developed from a primitive organic blob.

20. **Bible**: Man's body from the dust of the earth (Genesis 2:7)
Evolution: Man evolved from monkeys.

21. **Bible**: Man exercised dominion over all organisms (Genesis 1:28).
Evolution: Most organisms extinct before man existed.

22. **Bible**: Man originally a vegetarian (Genesis 1:29).
Evolution: Man originally a meat eater.

23. **Bible**: Fixed and distinct kinds (Genesis 1:11, 12, 21, 24, 25; I Corinthians 15:38-39).
Evolution: Life forms in a continual state of flux.

24. **Bible**: Man's sin the cause of death (Romans 5:12).
Evolution: Struggle and death existent long before the evolution of man.

In addition to these specific direct contradictions, there are stark differences of general principle between atheistic evolution and Biblical Christianity. Jesus said:

"A good tree cannot bring forth evil fruit, neither can a corrupt tree bring forth good fruit." (Matthew 7:18 KJV)

"The fruit of evolution has been all sorts of anti-Christian systems of belief and practice. It has served as an intellectual basis for Hitler's nazism and Marx's communism. It has prompted apostasy, atheism, secular humanism and libertinism, as well as establishing a basis for ethical relativism, which has spread through our society like a cancer. The mind and general welfare of mankind has suffered greatly as a result of this naturalistic philosophy.

According to the Bible, man is a responsible creature. One day he will give an account for his life's actions and motives. But when man is viewed as the product of some vague purposeless evolutionary process, he is conveniently freed from all moral obligations and responsibility. After all, he is merely an accident of nature, an intelligent animal at best." [25]

Evolution or creation: you cannot have both! Scott Huse's list is brutally clear. Look again at #14, for example. The Bible says in Genesis 1:20-31 that birds came on the fifth day and reptiles on the sixth day. That means birds came before reptiles. Yet evolution teaches as fact that reptiles came before birds. The two views are mutually exclusive. You either believe the Bible or you believe the speculations of men. Will you bow to science, or will you bow to your Creator? There are certain things in life that <u>are</u> black and white. We should have the integrity, especially as professing Christians, to choose God's Word and not the speculations of men.

---

[25] Scott Huse, *The Collapse of Evolution* (Grand Rapids: Baker Book House, 1983), p. 122-124.

You cannot be an evolutionist and believe the Bible as it is written. The plain word of Scripture is "God created". Therefore, evolution of molecules-to-man is a false speculation of man. Walter Brown reveals 57 irreconcilable differences between the Bible and "theistic" evolution in his book, In the Beginning, The Center for Scientific Creation, 5612 N. 20th Place, Phoenix, Arizona 85016, 1989, pp. 110-115.

MICRO VERSUS MACRO EVOLUTION

When speaking of evolution as a false speculation, we mean macroevolution -- one cell to man. What scientists call microevolution, obviously occurs. Microevolution is basically genetic variety within a certain kind of organism. For example, people are all different even though we come from one set of parents. How can five billion plus people vary so widely in appearance and abilities if we all come from the same set of parents? This is microevolution or adaption or, preferably, genetic variation, or perhaps, genetic drift. Even microevolution is not true evolution (something becoming something else due to changes in the genes). Different kinds of corn, dogs and mustard are still identified as corn, dogs and mustard. There is popcorn, sweet corn, and field corn; hounds, poodles and collies; many varieties of mustard. This does not prove evolution to be true. It only displays genetic differences within the families of corn, dogs, and mustard.

DIFFERENT KINDS OF PEOPLE

How might a creationist explain all the different races of people? God's record of the Tower of Babel incident in Genesis 11 provides the answer:

"And the whole earth was of one language, and of one speech.

And it came to pass, as they journeyed from the east, that they found a plain in the land of Shinar; and they dwelt there.

And they said one to another, "Come, let us make brick, and burn them thoroughly. And they had brick for stone, and slime had they for mortar.

And they said, "Come, let us build us a city and a tower, whose top may reach unto heaven; and let us make us a name, lest we be scattered abroad upon the face of the whole earth.

And the Lord came down to see the city and the tower, which the children of men builded.

And the Lord said, Behold, the people *is* one, and they have all one language; and this they begin to do: and now nothing will be restrained from them, which they have imagined to do.

Come, let us go down, and there confound their language, that they may not understand one another's speech.

So the Lord scattered them abroad from thence upon the face of all the earth: and they left off to build the city.

Therefore is the name of it called Babel; because the Lord did there confound the language of all the earth: and from thence did the Lord scatter them abroad upon the face of all the earth." (Genesis 11:1-9)

In the beginning, everyone spoke the same language. Therefore, they were able to pool their intellectual resources, since everyone could talk to everyone else. As a result, nothing was "impossible for them" or "restrained from them" (Genesis 11:6). They chose to violate God's command to scatter across the earth (Genesis 9:1), a violation which resulted in God creating the different basic languages. Only small populations of people isolated from other people groups could communicate with each other, and this would explain the "Cave Man" period as language restrictions and the chaos of the "scattering period" could certainly create some extremely isolated and primitive pockets of people.

The language restrictions forced them to disperse across the earth and "in-breed" with relatives. Certain races of people emerged after several generations of this inbreeding. [(God eventually proclaimed inbreeding to be sin in the law of Moses. Cain and Seth took wives from among their sisters but this was not sin until the Law came. See Leviticus 18 below.)

> **"Ye shall therefore keep my statutes, and my judgments: which if a man do, he shall live in them: I am the Lord.**
> **None of you shall approach to any that is near of kin to him, to uncover their nakedness: I am the Lord.**
> **The nakedness of thy father, or the nakedness of thy mother, shalt thou not uncover: she is thy mother; thou shalt not uncover her nakedness.**
> **The nakedness of thy father's wife shalt thou not uncover: it is thy father's nakedness.**
> **The nakedness of thy sister, the daughter of thy father, or daughter of thy mother, whether she be born at home, or born abroad, even their nakedness thou shalt not uncover..."**
> **(Leviticus 18:5ff).]**

Scientists tell us that all the races of mankind came from a single, female parent. On this point, Scripture does not negate "science". The races (variations within the human "kind") are most probably a result of the scattering of people around the globe by God after the Tower of Babel.

LANGUAGES DON'T BEGIN WITH GRUNTS

The study of language has developed into a complex field of scholarship. Linguists tell us that languages get more and more complex the farther back they trace them. The older ("more primitive") a language is, the more complex it appears to be. This is powerful evidence against evolution.

If evolution is true and man gradually evolved from more primitive creatures, language should get more and more simple the older it is said to be. Prehistoric man should have communicated first with grunts; then with single syllables; then with multi-syllabic words (ba-na-na); then, with sentence fragments, developing into sentences ("I want banana"), etc. What is found is just the opposite. Early languages such as Sumerian are so complex that only a handful of the most brilliant scholars can decipher them. The Tower of Babel incident explains the races and the problem of complex "primitive" languages. God created the languages instantly and fully mature. Evolution offers no good explanation for the complexity of the earliest known languages!

Linguistic researchers from around the world have published their ideas concerning the geographic location of our "primitive" mother tongue. Linguists call this language Proto-Indo-European. Two Russian experts, Thomas Gamkrelidze and Vyacheslav Ivanov, have offered evidence "...that Indo-European originated in an area known as Anatolia, which is now part of Turkey, and from there spread throughout Europe and the sub-continent." (see U.S. News and World Report, Nov. 5, 1990, page 62).

U.S. News and World Report was not the first publication to report that language can be traced back to Turkey. The Bible records for us that Noah and his family had their post-flood beginnings in Turkey:

> **"And the ark rested in the seventh month, on the seventeenth day of the month, upon the mountains of Ararat." (Genesis 8:4)**

Scientists trace language back to a particular place on earth, the Bible would describe that place to be the mountains of Ararat in Turkey. The linguists agree!

BABEL AND HI-TECH SCIENCE

Since the creation of languages at the Tower of Babel, the endeavors of generations of mankind have been limited (not able to do the impossible) by the language barrier. But now, for the first time since the Tower of Babel, our generation has a common international language -- the language of hi-tech computers. With computers, we can again pool our international research and knowledge and do the impossible (man on the moon, heart transplants, Concorde jet travel, etc.). God stepped into time to stop this situation in Genesis 11. What might He do in our generation as the teachings of evolution convince more and more people that God is not necessary for any part of our existence? We are rapidly becoming a people who believe the bottom line of William Henley's Invictus: "I am the master of my fate, I am the captain of my soul." This was the attitude of Babylon, and the Creator was not pleased.

One other thought to consider in Genesis 11 -- could the people of Babel have been building a water-proof tower? The biblical text states the use of specially fired bricks (hardened) and the use of water-proof tar (KJV "slime") for mortar. The flood judgment of Noah's day would have been fresh on the minds of these people. Could they have been shaking their fists at God (rebelling) with their pooled intellectual resources as they built a water-proof tower, thus making a statement? "God, you can't get us again with a flood! We will all come together in our water-proof tower that reaches into the sky. We will save our own lives in spite of You. We will control our destiny. We will take charge of our lives." How much of this attitude is like Lucifer -- **"I will be like the Most High"**? (Isaiah 14:13,14) The science of that day may have convinced the people that they could quite satisfactorily live apart from their Creator. Scientists today climb into their ivory towers and say in their hearts and in their papers: "There is no God. We can do quite well without Him. We are all gods and control our own destiny."

EVOLUTION AND THE SCIENTIFIC METHOD

Scientists often make proclamations and publish papers that elevate them to god-like status. Are we forced to believe that science and the scientific method have "toppled" God? From our earliest school days, we are taught that science is based on careful experimentation and disciplined thought. Science gives us facts. We can trust it. We are further educated by television programs and interviews with Ph.D.'s like Carl Sagan stating that "evolution is no longer a theory, but a proven fact". <u>This is not the scientific method!</u> Evolutionist, Hy Ruchlis, defines the scientific method:

> "The Scientific Method is the basic set of procedures that scientists use for obtaining new knowledge about the universe in which we live." [26]

Making a proclamation that evolution is no longer a theory, but a proven fact is just that -- a proclamation. It is not testable science. It does not fit within the definition of the Scientific Method. Ruchlis continues:

> <u>"Unless the teachings of the authorities on a subject are based upon scientific method, error can be just as easily transmitted as fact...</u>
> The most important point to remember about the method of science is that it rests upon the attitude of <u>open mind</u>. In accordance with this attitude, one has the right to question <u>any</u> accepted fact. One who searches for truth has to learn to question

---

[26] Hy Ruchlis, *Discovering Scientific Method* (N.Y.: Harper & Row, 1963), p. 7.

deeply the things that are generally accepted as being "obviously true." [27]

How does evolution as a "scientific" explanation for origins measure up under Ruchlis' explanation of scientific method? It receives a failing grade. Could evolution be "error... transmitted as fact"? It certainly could. Do evolutionists present an "open mind"? Do they permit their classroom students to question evolution as perhaps not being "...obviously true"? On the contrary, evolutionists have amply demonstrated they want only one view taught in the classrooms of the world.

When a credentialed scientist who is a creationist presents hard evidence to support the Creator and His creation, he or she is accused of teaching religion.

But evolution from one cell to man is not based on the scientific method[28] and is therefore a faith system. That means it is just as "religious" as belief in special creation. The question is not, "is evolution, science and creation a religion?" but "which system of belief -- creation or evolution -- has the most factual science to back it up?"

David E. Green (Institute for Enzyme Research, University of Wisconsin, Madison) and Robert F. Goldberger (National Institutes of Health, Bethesda, Maryland) have studied the scientific method and its relationship to the processes of evolution. Their studied opinion is that macroevolution is beyond the range of

---

[27] ibid: Ruchlis, pp. 7,8.

[28] "The open mind is one important aspect of the scientific attitude which lies at the base of scientific method. A person who approaches a problem with a closed mind, unwilling to examine new facts, without any desire to make careful observations, and subject to the tyranny of certainty, has little or no chance of solving that problem properly. But a person with scientific attitudes, who knows how easy it is to be wrong, who examines new facts even if they seem to contradict his pet beliefs, who actually goes out hunting for such facts -- such a person has a head start along the road to the solution of any problem he faces." ibid: Ruchlis, p. 11.

"testable hypothesis". In other words, it is not able to be proven factually true with the scientific method. The origin of the first living cell is scientifically "unknowable". In spite of this, evolutionists Green and Goldberger[29] deny the existence of anything supernatural ("paraphysical"). Contrary to the thinking of these two scientists, <u>evolution is not science: it is religion</u>. Yet religious evolutionists are not willing to let religious creationists present their views in the public schcol system. In fact, as we all know, our courts here in America ("The land of the free and the home of the brave") will not allow an alternative view for the origin of man to be presented in our classrooms without some sort of objection. If creation is so obviously an absurd option for belief, one would certainly have to question why it is such a threatening concept to consider in the classrooms of our children. Surely, if evolution is true and as easily validated as scientists contend, there should be no threat at all in allowing it to be challenged by the option of creation.

It is interesting to note that a growing number of evolutionary scientists are realizing that there is a gross lack of scientific evidence to support the molecules-to-man evolution model. The gnawing reality is that, as one evolutionist has stated: "The creationists seem to have the better argument."

---

[29] "...the macromolecule-to-cell transition is a jump of fantastic dimensions, which lies beyond the range of testable hypothesis. In this area, all is conjecture. The available facts do not provide a basis for postulating that cells arose on this planet.

This is not to say that some paraphysical forces were at work. We simply wish to point out the fact that there is no scientific evidence. The physicist has learned to avoid trying to specify when time began and when matter was created, except within the framework for frank speculation. The origin of the precursor cell appears to fall into the same category of unknowables."David E. Green (Institute for Enzyme Research, University of Wisconsin, Madison, U.S.A.) and Robert F. Goldberger (National Institutes of Health, Bethesda, Maryland, U.S.A.), *Molecular Insights into the Living Process* (New York: Academic Press, 1967), pp. 406-407, quoted from *The Quote Book*, p. 20.

THE LORD WILL PREVAIL

When one religion is in competition with another religion, the true religion will <u>ultimately</u> prevail. The God of creation is already the victor. An anonymous writer, M.B., who works for the Environmental Protection Agency (E.P.A.) expressed it this way:

"God created the Heaven and the Earth. Quickly He was faced with a class action suit for failure to file an environmental impact statement. He was granted a temporary permit for the heavenly part of the project, but was stymied with a cease and desist order for the earthly part.

Appearing at the hearing, God was asked why He began His earthly project in the first place. He replied that He just liked to be creative!

Then God said, "Let there be light" and immediately the officials demanded to know how the light would be made. Would there be strip mining? What about thermal pollution? God explained that the light would come from a huge ball of fire. God was granted permission to make light, assuming that no smoke would result from the ball of fire, and to conserve energy, the light would have to be out half of the time. God agreed and said He would call the light "Day" and the darkness, "Night". The officials replied that they were not interested in semantics.

God said, "Let the Earth bring forth green herb and such as may seed." The Environmental Protection Agency agreed so long as native seed was used. Then God said, "Let the waters bring forth the creeping creatures having life; and the fowl that may fly over the Earth." Officials pointed out that this would require the approval of the Game and Fish Commission coordinated with the Heavenly Wildlife Federation and the Audubongelic Society.

Everything was okay until God said He wanted to complete the project in six days. Officials said that it would take at least 100 days to review the application and impact statement. After that there would be a public hearing. Then there would be 10 to 12 months before...

At this point, God created hell!"

Evolution may be winning some tactical skirmishes in teamwork with the world system, but let us never forget that our Lord will have the last word. The Creator tells us how everything will conclude in Philippians 2:10,11:

> **"That at the name of Jesus every knee should bow, of** _things_ **in heaven, and** _things_ **in earth, and** _things_ **under the earth;**
> **And** _that_ **every tongue should confess that Jesus Christ** _is_ **Lord, to the glory of God the Father."** (emphasis added)

Our Lord, our Creator is the Victor! Isaac Asimov, Carl Sagan, Ernst Mayr, and Stephen Jay Gould, as well as that evolutionist college professor or school teacher, will <u>all</u> bow down before their Savior and Creator, Jesus Christ the Lord. They will confess out loud with their own tongue, "Jesus Christ is Lord", to the glory of God the Father. They have examined the creation and have <u>willfully chosen to believe a lie</u>. Unless they come to the Lord Jesus in simple faith and confess their sinful rebellion against Him, they will "bow" and "confess" at the judgment to no avail. They will stand before God their Creator without excuse. Romans 1:19-23 says:

> **"Because that which may be known of God is manifest in them; for God hath shewed it unto them.**
> **For the invisible things of him from the creation of the world are clearly seen, being understood by the things that are made, even his eternal power and Godhead; so that they are without excuse.**
> **Because that, when they knew God, they glorified** _him_ **not as God, neither were thankful; but became vain in their imaginations, and their foolish heart was darkened.**
> **Professing themselves to be wise, they became fools,**
> **And changed the glory of the uncorruptible God into an image made like to corruptible man, and to birds and four-footed beasts and creeping things." (Romans 1:19-23)**

The great evolutionary minds of the day have a tendency to elevate man and creature to the status of God. From chemicals to man, all is essentially equal. All is "One"! But is this wisdom or is it foolishness? God says:

> **"The fear of the Lord is the beginning of wisdom: And the knowledge of the Holy One is understanding."** (Proverbs 9:10)

True wisdom is belief in God the Creator. There is unity and there is diversity in His creation. Man might look like a monkey and even act like a monkey, but he cannot take a blood transfusion from a monkey. As professing Christians, when we fail to bow before God in recognition of His sovereignty and omnipotence, we open ourselves to being tainted with vain philosophies and the foolish speculations of this world system. Have we so devoted ourselves to learning the ways of the world that we have neglected the ways of the Word? Do we stand condemned before our Creator because our true commitment lies with the imaginations and speculations of men rather than with the eternal truths of the Bible? Are we lacking faith because we have drifted into subjecting the Bible to science instead of subjecting science to the Bible? Truly **"there is a way which seemeth right unto a man, but the end thereof are the ways of death"**. (Proverbs 14:12) "O God, help us with our unbelief!"

MARVEL OF GOD'S CREATION #3

The Black and Yellow Garden Spider

The black and yellow garden spider is a special creation of the God of the Bible. As does each species of spider, it has its own unique web, which may be spun more than two feet in diameter. At the center of the web, the spider makes a dense area of silk that often gives the appearance of a zipper or zig-zag bulk of silk.

The female weaves an egg-sac that is pear-shaped and about one inch in diameter. She then hangs the egg sac somewhere close to her main web.

"This spider lays all her eggs at once. There are usually 40 or 50. As each egg is expelled the female dusts it with a powdery substance. This dusting gives the egg a coating that looks like the bloom on a plum or a grape.

The eggs are enclosed in a silken cup at the center of the sac. The cup, in turn, is covered by a layer of flossy silk. And for additional protection the female weaves another layer of silk around both the cup and the floss. This outer covering is tightly woven and brown in color.

Shortly after the eggs are laid they hatch. The young are known as spiderlings. They break out of the shells by means of an organ known as the "egg tooth". This later disappears." [30]

---

[30] Will Barker, *Winter-Sleeping Wildlife* (New York: Harper and Row, Pubs., 1958), pp. 94-96.

The black and yellow garden spider is like a miniature manufacturing plant. It produces different kinds of webbing in more than one color for different purposes, as well as making the powdery substance with which it coats its eggs. Some of its webbing is sticky to entrap insects for food. Other parts of the web are not sticky, enabling the spider to move rapidly across the web without ensnaring itself. How does evolution (the impersonal plus time plus chance) explain the complicated ability of one spider to produce different types of webbing for different purposes and even in different colors (varying from white to brown)? And how does evolution explain the presence of an "egg tooth" in a baby spider?

When the spider decides it is time to move on to new territory, it has an ingenious means of travel:

> "To reach new locations the spider travels by a means of transportation known as "ballooning". A spiderling or spider throws out streams of silk. These threads form a sort of "flying carpet." It rises on warm currents of ascending air, and spiders and spiderlings are borne aloft and scattered far and wide.
>
> Sometimes they go as high as 14,000 to 15,000 feet and travel hundreds or even thousands of miles." [31]

Spiders undergo several moults before they are fully grown. If they do not shed their skin, they die. How would the spider know this until it grew too big for its shell and died? Dead spiders do not evolve new abilities!

The skin moults and splits open in a special manner. First, the spider injects a certain liquid called "moulting fluid" between his outer old skin and his newly developing skin. Where does this special fluid come from, and how does

---

[31] Ibid: Will Barker, p. 96.

the spider know what to do with it and when to use it? Using the moulting fluid too soon or too late is fatal!

The way that the old skin splits is crucial. If it cracks open in the wrong places, or at wrong angles, the spider perishes.

> "Once the old skin is sufficiently loose, splits appear along the sides of the body and in front of the eyes. But no horizontal split occurs across the body. The vertical split along each side of the body and the one crosswise in front of the eyes form a flap of skin.
>
> The spider pushes up the flap like a man thrusting up a hinged trap door. It pushes and pushes and pushes until the flap drops back over the abdomen. Out of the opening wriggles the spider." [32]

What infinite care our Creator-God has taken in the design of the spider! This little creature breaks the rules of the evolution model with its marvelous complexity.   It needed God to create it just like it is with all its abilities and peculiarities. The black and yellow garden spider is a marvel of God's creation -- the God for whom nothing is impossible (see Luke 1:37), and who daily lives to make intercession for us (Romans 8:34) and who loves us so much that He willingly gave His life for us (John 3:16).

---

[32] Ibid: Will Barker, p. 97.

4

"MISSING LINKS" ARE MISSING

As a college student I was convinced that evolution was true and that, in time, scientists would find the missing pieces. I thought science would ultimately provide us with an unbroken chain of evidence supporting the evolution and relationship of all things. Many scientists are still hoping for this evidence. However, Stephen Jay Gould, Professor of Geology and Paleontology at Harvard, believes that the unbroken chain of evolutionary evidence will never be found -- that what we see in the fossils and in living creatures is more accurately explained with the creation model. Gould is still an evolutionist, but he writes:

"The birds of Massachusetts and the bugs in my backyard are unambiguous members of species recognized in the same way by all experienced observers.

This notion of species as "natural kinds"...fit splendidly with creationist tenets....

But how could a division of the organic world into discrete entities be justified by an evolutionary theory that proclaimed ceaseless change as the fundamental fact of nature?" [33]

Dr. Gould is making a statement about what we see as opposed to what evolution theorizes we ought to be seeing. We see discrete entities, distinct species. In the fossil record, there are fish, turtles and cockroaches. They are individually distinct, identifiable creatures. In life, we can also see fish, turtles and cockroaches. We can identify them. They are not 1/2 fish and 1/2 turtle or 1/2 turtle and 1/2 cockroach. We do not see elephants evolving fins or whales evolving wings. The discrete entities we see in the fossil record and in life are not "questionable" species. They are not transitional forms, as evolution would require. This is a problem for the evolutionist. If evolution is true, creatures should not be so easily identifiable. Every creature should be difficult to categorize, classify and name, if evolution is correct (and life is "evolving along"). Could it be that evolution is not correct? That each animal is easily identifiable (as giraffe or beetle or fish or turtle or cockroach) truly does "fit splendidly with creationist tenets." Ceaseless change in the fossils or living plants and animals does not appear to be "...the fundamental fact of nature".[34] (Emphasis added).

GOD CREATED KINDS

---

[33] Stephen Jay Gould, "A Quahog is a Quahog," *Natural History*, Vol. 88 (7), August-September, 1979, p. 18.

[34] ibid.

God tells us He created each plant and animal after its own kind (Genesis 1:11, 12, 21, 24, 25). Nothing evolved from some lower life form and nothing is presently evolving into a higher life form. From a creationist position, what we see in the fossil record and in life is exactly what we would expect to see. The lack of transitional forms is why evolutionists have the "missing link" problem, although some deny this. The "missing links" are <u>missing</u>. They are completely absent in the fossil record and in living organisms. They never will be found. God created each plant and animal after its own kind, therefore, you would not expect to see "missing links".

"MISSING LINKS" OR "UNBROKEN TIES"

The evolutionist's propaganda machine constantly barrages us through public TV, magazines and newspapers with broad ambiguities and undocumented claims supporting evolutionary theory. A letter in the <u>Dallas Morning News</u> by Drs. Alvin and Joel Taurog of Southwestern Medical School exemplifies this type of propaganda:

> "Biological evolution asserts that all living organisms are interrelated by unbroken ties of genealogy. Although referred to as a theory, evolution is as much a fact as anything discovered by science, as well confirmed as the rotation of the planets around the sun or the roundness of the earth. The concept of evolution is central to biology and a massive body of evidence corroborates the evolutionary origin of all living organisms, including humans. While much remains to be learned regarding the mechanisms of evolution, the evolution of species is accepted by biologists as proven fact." [35]

---

[35] Drs. Alvin and Joel Taurog, *Dallas Morning News,* March 6, 1987, Letters to the Editor.

Let us evaluate this paragraph of Drs. Taurog. If "...all living organisms are interrelated by unbroken ties of genealogy", then the leading evolutionary thinker of Harvard, Dr. Stephen Jay Gould, is wrong. Gould states:

> "The absence of fossil evidence for intermediary stages between major transitions in organic design, indeed our inability, even in our imagination, to construct functional intermediates in many cases, has been a persistent and nagging problem for gradualistic accounts of evolution." [36]

"Gradualistic evolution" means evolution of one creature into a more sophisticated and more complex creature over long periods of time. One creature gradually becomes another if given enough time. Gradualistic evolution, if true, should have evidence of transitional intermediate life forms in fossils and in living animals. Gould continues:

> "All paleontologists know that the fossil record contains precious little in the way of intermediate forms; transitions between major groups are characteristically abrupt." [37]

What Gould is saying is that the missing links remain missing. There are no transitional (in-between) forms. No plant or animal is evolving into a higher form as far as the fossils can confirm.

---

[36] Stephen Jay Gould, "Is a New and General Theory of Evolution Emerging?", *Paleobiology*, Vol. 6 (1), January, 1980, p. 127, as quoted in *The Quote Book*, p. 8.

[37] Stephen Jay Gould, "The Return of Hopeful Monsters," *Natural History*, Vol. LXXVI (6), June-July, 1977, p. 24. Quoted in *The Quote Book*, p. 8.

"SUNRISE" OR "EARTH TURN"

Where are these "unbroken ties" referred to by Drs. Taurog? They present no scientific evidence to support their view. The evidence is only implied. They do appear to erect a "straw-man-creationist" and to take a few sideways swipes at him. In mentioning the "rotation of the planets around the sun or the roundness of the earth" as true science, are they implying that the Bible and creationists believe in the "sun rising on a flat earth"? How accurate are these doctors in the use of language? Do they say to a patient, "Did you see the beautiful <u>sunrise</u> this morning?" Or would they be scientifically accurate and ask "Did you see the beautiful <u>earth turn</u> this morning?" The Bible uses common, ordinary language. That the earth is not flat, but a sphere is taught in Isaiah 40:22: **"It is He that sitteth upon (above) the circle of the earth..." (KJV)**. The Bible teaches that as God looks down upon earth, it appears as a sphere or circle. Psalm 19 (New American Standard Version) is a scripture that uses normal language and refers to the sun rising. The Bible is not inaccurate because it uses common figures of speech.

Where can we find the "massive body of evidence (that) corroborates the evolutionary origin of all living creatures, including humans" (as Drs. Taurog allege)? The "massive body of evidence" proving the evolution of man would not fill a single casket according to evolutionist and prolific author Dr. Lyall Watson:

> "The fossils that decorate our family tree are so scarce that there are still more scientists than specimens.

The remarkable fact is that all the physical evidence we have for human evolution can still be placed, with room to spare, inside a single coffin!" [38]

Drs. Alvin and Joel Taurog say still more:

"When religion and science come into conflict, it is generally in the realm of belief....Scientific belief is based solely upon evidence that is validated by observation, experiment and prediction; neither religious belief, nor any other belief system, is subject to these constraints." [39]

Apparently, Drs. Taurog believe that the evolution model of one cell to man is science and thus can be validated with the scientific method. Creation science is apparently religious belief in their view. They add, "The interrelationships among living organisms from microbes to man have never been clearer,..." It is not clear precisely what these doctors are referring to, but from the smallest life forms to the largest, from the simplest to the most complex, there is no scientific evidence to prove that they (small to large or simple to complex) are related as ancestors to or progeny from each other. Natural History of May 1977 (p. 14) published the words of Dr. Stephen Jay Gould:

"The extreme rarity of transitional forms in the fossil record persists as the trade secret of paleontology. The evolutionary trees that adorn our textbooks have data only at the tips and nodes of their branches; the rest is inference, however reasonable, not the evidence of fossils... We fancy ourselves as the only true students of life's history, yet to preserve our favored account of evolution by natural selection we view our data as so bad that we never see the very process we profess to study."

---

[38] Dr. Lyall Watson, "The Water People," *Science Digest*, Vol. 90, May, 1982, p. 44.

[39] Drs. Alvin and Joel Taurog, *Dallas Morning News*, March 6, 1987, Letters to the Editor.

MOLECULAR BIOLOGY DISPROVES EVOLUTION

Even at the level of molecules, evidence to support evolution is lacking. In chapter 2, we discussed the fact that at the cellular level of living creatures there are important differences that distinguish between basic kinds of flesh. For instance, the cells that make up the flesh of birds and fish are not the same. Scientists are studying even smaller entities than cells as they examine the molecules of the cell. This field of study is named Molecular Biology.

A book that every Christian family (and non-Christian, as well) should have is, Of Pandas and People: The Central Question of Biological Origins. Written by creationists as a supplemental high school biology textbook supporting the view that life demands a designer, this book deals with the molecular evidence for creation.

"The study of living things on the molecular level is a relatively new field. The information that scientists derive from molecular biology may be used to compare and categorize organisms, a field known as *biochemical taxonomy*. Biochemical analysis holds out the promise of making taxonomy a more precise science, because it allows differences between various organisms to be quantified and measured....

Proponents of intelligent design read similarity in structure as a reflection of similarity in function. All living organisms must survive in the same universe and must fit its ecological web. All must fit into a food chain. The need to function within a common universe puts common physical and chemical requirements on all organisms. It would be both logical and efficient for an intelligent agent to design living things with a common biochemical base....

The significant new contribution biochemistry offers is a mathematically quantifiable means of determining how similar classes of organisms are. But when several similarities are put side by side, <u>the pattern that emerges contradicts all expectations based on evolution</u>." [40] (Emphasis added).

Animals that evolutionists have always believed to be closely related in the evolutionary chain are now known to be unrelated when studied at the molecular level. Kenyon and Davis continue:

> "To use classic evolutionary terminology, amphibians are intermediate between fish and the other land-dwelling vertebrates. Yet, analysis of their amino acids does not place amphibians in an intermediate position. This is true no matter what species of amphibian we choose for comparison. Based upon the evolutionary series, we would expect some amphibians to be closer to fish ("primitive" species) and others to be closer to reptiles ("advanced" species). But this is not the case. No matter which species are taken as the basis for comparison, the distance between amphibians and fish, or between amphibians and reptiles, is always the same....
>   The revolution in molecular biology has given us new, mathematically quantifiable data on the similarities in living things. But <u>the data have served to support a picture of the organic world consistent with the theory of intelligent design</u>." [41]

(Emphasis added).

Author Michael Denton [*Evolution: A Theory in Crisis* (Harper and Row, 1986)], a Ph.D. in molecular biology (who is not a creationist as far as I know), argues that evolution from one cell to man is not indicated at the level of the molecule. After looking at molecules for evidence for "missing links" between the different classes of creatures, Denton writes (p. 286):

> "There is a total absence of partially inclusive or intermediate classes, and therefore none of the groups

---

[40] Percival Davis and Dean H. Kenyon, *Of Pandas and People* (Dallas: Haughton Publishing Co., 1989), pp. 34-36.

[41] ibid, pp. 37,38.

traditionally cited by evolutionary biologists as intermediate gives even the slightest hint of a supposedly transitional character."

Of course, if there is no evidence for evolutionary relationships at the level of molecules, which are the basic building blocks of nature, then the idea of evolution of enzymes, proteins, plasma and tissue is totally absurd. The Bible says:

For thus says the Lord, who created the heavens
(He is the God who formed the earth and made it,
He established it and did not create it a waste place,
But formed it to be inhabited).
I am the Lord, and there is none else...
And there is no other God besides Me,
A righteous God and a Savior;
There is none except Me. (Isaiah 45:18,21b)

Dr. Vincent Sarich, an evolutionist and Professor at the University of California at Berkeley, did a series of studies at the molecular level on the evolution of man. At first, his studies were scorned by his evolutionary colleagues. He had the audacity to announce in 1967 that Ramapithecus (proclaimed by Elwyn Simons and David Pilbeam of Yale to be one of the earliest ancestors of man) was not at all ancestral to man, but more probably an ancestor to the orangutan.

"The year was 1967. Sarich and his partner, Allan Wilson, were comparing blood proteins from human beings, chimpanzees and gorillas -- finding them remarkably similar. After analyzing the slight differences, they decided that the ancestors of human beings must have diverged from those of the African apes only about 5 million years ago, instead of the 20 million to 30 million years that fossil evidence seemed to suggest.

Their conclusion was regarded by many paleontologists as heresy. It was bad enough that Sarich and Wilson were challenging the conventional estimate of the age of the human

line. Worse, they were doing it with test tubes and biochemistry -
- all but ignoring the fossils on which so much evolutionary
theory was based. Most experts then believed that human beings
could trace their ancestry at least as far back as a 14 million-year-
old creature called Ramapithecus, and paleontologist Elwyn
Simons, then of Yale, spoke for many of his colleagues when he
pronounced the Sarich-Wilson work "impossible to believe."

Times have changed.   While Simons still thinks
Ramapithecus may be a human ancestor, he has little company.
New fossil discoveries have convinced many experts that the
animal was ancestral to the orangutan." [42]

Molecular research is eliminating the supposed
evolutionary ancestors of people, one by one.

---

[42] Kevin McKean, "Preaching the Molecular Gospel," *Discover*, Vol. 4 (7),
July, 1983, p. 34.

MARVEL OF GOD'S CREATION #4
The Gecko Lizard
AND
The Human Ear

These two marvels of God's creation are included not only to display God's incredible designs in His creatures, but also to acquaint you more fully with the type of information you can glean from the creationist magazine, <u>Creation Ex Nihilo</u>. The following are articles in <u>Creation Ex Nihilo</u> magazine Vol. 14, No. 4 of September - November 1992 (published by Creation Science Foundation Ltd., P.O. Box 302, Sunnybank, QLD, 4109, Australia), by Robert Kofahl, Ph.D., and Tom Wagner. In my opinion every family should subscribe to <u>Creation Ex Nihilo</u>!

Dr. Robert Kofahl teaches us about the gecko lizard on page 6.

"A Lizard on Your Ceiling"

"The gecko lizard can walk across your ceiling upside down without falling off. How does it do this?

Until a few years ago scientists did not know, though they proposed several conflicting theories. Examination of the toe-pads of the gecko with optical microscopes at up to 2,000 diameters magnification revealed thousands of little fibres arranged like the tufts of bristles in a toothbrush. Yet the question remained unanswered. An answer was finally provided by the powerful scanning electron microscope, which was able to take a series of remarkable photographs magnified to 35,000 diameters and more.

What was revealed?

The gecko has on its toe pads many millions of fine fibres tipped with little suction cups, each about eight millionths of an inch in diameter. In conjunction with this, the lizard's feet are designed so that the tips of the toes bend or curl upward so that he can peel off the suction cups gradually at each step and not get himself too firmly stuck to the surface. It is estimated that the gecko has at least 500 million suction cups on his toes.

The extraordinary microscopic structure of the gecko lizard's toe pads clearly indicates intelligent purposeful design. No remotely plausible scheme for the origin of the gecko's suction cups by random mutations and natural selection has yet been proposed by evolutionary theorists.   And should some scientist with a clever imagination succeed in devising such a scheme, he would still be without a scrap of fossil evidence to demonstrate that the hypothetical process of evolution actually took place in the past."

"-- You can't see with the naked eye the tiny suction cups on a gecko's foot. But each chevron-shaped ridge on the gecko's amazing foot pad is composed of millions of fibres tipped with microscopic suction cups. This allows it to walk upside down across your ceiling, or sideways across your wall --."

With such marvelous evidence of a designer, how can anyone doubt the existence of God?

In the same issue of <u>Creation Ex Nihilo,</u> Tom Wagner composed a "Think Spot" detailing some specifics concerning the human ear (page 13):

"Your Hearing: A powerful pointer to God's creation"

"Contemplation of the size of things that have been created can be a very effective tool in comprehending the greatness of God. For example, consider the Creator's technical ability in a study of human hearing. The ability of our ears to detect sound is much greater than the minimum expected requirement for survival had man simply evolved.

In a book edited by David Lipscomb, 1988, <u>Hearing Conservation in Industry, Schools, and the Military</u>, we read on page 303:

'The ear is capable of sensory response to sound whose pressure at the ear drum is no greater than two ten-thousandths of a millionth of barometric pressure. This pressure moves the ear drum about one one-hundred-millionth of an inch. That dimension is approximately one one-hundredth the width of a hydrogen molecule, the tiniest of all known molecules. Therefore, throughout a significant portion of the ear's dynamic range, it is moving in sub-molecular dimensions.'

To visually grasp the incredible sensitivity Lipscomb describes, imagine what it would be like to watch a six-foot man, standing on the surface of the earth, shrink to only one one-hundred-millionth of an inch. The earth, shrinking also - but still enormous when compared to the man - would proportionately reduce to a tiny ball no bigger than the small letter 'o' on this page! The man would become utterly invisible, even to the powerful microscopes of today.

Given this example, a person can begin to appreciate the way God has created the incomprehensibly tiny, as well as the unimaginably large things of this universe. It also helps us to consider the miracle of hearing with which our Creator has blessed us. Something we should thank Him for. After all, 'Faith cometh by hearing...'

So praise be to God for what He has done!"

5

ORANGUTANS, MONKEYS AND MAN

When studied at the level of molecules, cells, or fossil bones, the evolutionary ancestors of people (ape-man or man-like-apes) are not to be found. In spite of this, elaborate attempts are made to "prove" that man evolved from early primates (ape-like creatures).

In the late sixties and early seventies, much of the scientific community ruled Ramapithecus (an ape-like creature) ancestral to the orangutan or to an ape, instead of its original position as ancestral to humans. When considering Ramapithecus in 1973, Alan Walker and Peter Andrews wrote their belief that the jaw of Ramapithecus was that of a true ape (Nature, Vol. 244, 1973, p. 313).

Yet, in 1982, the son of Louis and Mary Leakey, who are world famous pioneers in the study of "prehistoric" man, stated:

> "Ramapithecines are thought to be the group from which our ancestors evolved." [43]

PILTDOWN MAN

If Ramapithecus appears in school or college textbooks as part of the evolution of man, it can be discarded, as should the Piltdown man, which was shown to be a hoax in 1953.[44] Piltdown's filed teeth and bone had been stained to make it appear to be ancient.

Fourteen years after Piltdown Man was proven by the evolutionary scientific community to be a total fake and bad joke, Harvard University Press published these words (admittedly this is a long quote, but I include it to display how far the evolutionary community will go to support their insupportable claims even years after one of their "evidences" has been proven to be a fraud):

> "Unlike all other fossil men is *Eoanthropus*, known from a fragmentary skull and the right half of a lower jaw with two teeth, the first and second molars, in place. The specimens were obtained by Mr. William Dawson from a small opening by the roadside at Piltdown, Sussex, England, and described by Sir Arthur Smith Woodward. It is difficult to determine their age, for

---

[43] Richard E. Leakey, *Human Origins*, Lodestar Books (New York: E.P. Dutton, 1982), p. 20. For much information about fossil-man from a creationist perspective please read: <u>Bones of Contention</u> by Marvin Lubenow (Baker Books: Grand Rapids) 1992. Also: <u>The Illustrated Origins Answer Book</u> by Paul S. Taylor (Eden Productions, P.O. Box 41644 Mesa, AZ   85274-1644) 1992.

[44] See *The Hominid Gang: Behind the Scenes in the Search for Human Origins* by Delta Willis, with an introduction by Stephen Jay Gould (New York: Viking Press, 1989), p. 24. See also *The Piltdown Man* by Ronald Millar (New York: St. Martin's Press, 1972), front cover slip.

fragments of mammals characteristic of the Pliocene and Pleistocene are mingled in the river-borne gravel. If contemporaneous with the most modern of them, Piltdown man was probably not more recent than the third interglacial stage, since *Hippopotamus* and other subtropical animals occur with it.

The skull is so fragmentary that those who have studied it have been unable to agree as to the proper reconstruction: estimates of its cranial capacity have varied from 1079 cc. to 1500 cc. , and an intermediate figure of about 1300 cc. has finally been reached. It is not at all of the Neanderthal type, but has a high forehead like that of modern man. Aside from the fact that the bones are exceedingly thick, it is not peculiar. The jaw, however, is admitted by all to be more like that of a chimpanzee than like that of any man, living or extinct. This was recognized in the original description. The two teeth are like human molars, but the remainder of the jaw affords too much space to be filled by ordinary teeth. Hence, in his restoration of the anterior part, Smith Woodward made the canines large, like those of a chimpanzee, and allowed for a small diastema. The correctness of his view was demonstrated in a striking way the year after publication, when Dawson and Father Teilhard de Chardin, who were resifting the gravel at the spot where the jaw was found, found a large canine. It is twice as large as that of a man and almost exactly like that of a modern chimpanzee. This association seemed to many to be an unnatural one, so the jaw was attributed by some to a species of chimpanzee. The later finding of a few more fragments at a near-by site seems, however, to have convinced most of those interested that skull and jaw belong together. *Eoanthropus dawsoni* (Piltdown man), then is to some people the missing link between man and the apes. The forehead is high, the brow ridge insignificant, and the brain large, all features of man, but the chinless jaw has the big canines of an ape." [45]

Thus as late as 1967, the prestigious Harvard University Press was still promoting the Piltdown Hoax as a possible "...missing link between man and the apes", when it had been proven a sham nearly fifteen years earlier.

---

[45] Percy E. Raymond, Prehistoric Life (Cambridge: Harvard University Press, 1969) pp. 282, 283.

NEBRASKA MAN

Nebraska man was formed from a single tooth found in 1922. In 1924, the skull was found and the tooth fit perfectly in the empty socket -- it was a pig's tooth! [46]

NEANDERTHAL AND CRO-MAGNON

We might also add that Neanderthal and Cro-magnon man are now believed to be normal European Homosapiens. Some of these "prehistoric men" have a larger brain cavity than modern man.

Dr. Percy E. Raymond of Harvard University, states in regard to Neanderthal:

> "In actual capacity, the cranial cavity was larger than that of the average European, some skulls measuring 1,600 cc." [47]

Donald Johanson, one of the world's most recognized experts on "fossil man", writes:

> "...Neanderthal Man. He was another *Homo*. Some think he was the same species as ourselves....
>
> I consider Neanderthal nonspecific with *sapiens*, with myself. One hears talk about putting him in a business suit and turning him loose in the subway. It is true; one could do it, and he would never be noticed. He was just a little heavier-boned than people of today, more primitive in a few facial features. But he was a man. His brain was as big as modern man's, but shaped in a slightly different way. Could he make change at the subway booth and recognize a token? He certainly could." [48]

---

[46] See *The Hominid Gang*, p. 22. Also W. R. Bird's <u>The Origin of Species Revisited</u> (Regency: Nashville) Vol. 1, pp. 227,228. (1991).

[47] Raymond, p. 281.

[48] Donald C. Johanson and Maitland A. Edey, *Lucy: The Beginnings of Humankind* (New York: Simon and Schuster, 1981), p. 20.

According to evolutionist Johanson, Neanderthal is not prehistoric man, not some ancient evolutionary ancestor, but just like us, modern man!

PEKING MAN

Peking Man has been categorized as Homo erectus. He disappeared during World War II. There is not a single bone left of Peking Man, although books have been written about the international search for the "bones".

An entertaining and readable book on the search for Peking Man was written by Christopher Janus with William Brashler, entitled, The Search for Peking Man. Mentioned in the book as one of the people who aided in the discovery of Peking Man is Teilhard De Chardin -- one of the perpetrators of the Piltdown Man hoax! [49]   Since De Chardin was implicated in the Piltdown hoax and managed to involve himself with Peking man as well, how can we be certain that the documentation we have of Peking man is reliable?

Janus records the total number of Peking Man fossil fragments before the Japanese invasion of China:

"... they labeled, described, photographed and categorized the casts of the 175 fossil fragments that had been collected" [50]

Peking Man supposedly consisted of:

"...5 skulls, about 150 jaw fragments and teeth, 9 thigh bones and fragments, 2 upper arm bones, a collar bone, and a wrist bone" [51]

---

[49] Christopher Janus, *The Search for Peking Man* (New York: MacMillan Pub. Co., Inc., 1975), p. 31.

[50] Ibid, p. 30.

[51] Ibid, p. 32.

All these bones have disappeared! Apparently, the evolutionary scientists cannot even agree on how many bones represented Peking Man. Johanson records:

> "...5 skulls, 15 smaller pieces of the skull or face, 14 lower jaws and 152 teeth." [52]

So there is no hard evidence that Peking Man is an ancestor of Homo sapiens. Some photographs of Peking skulls remain. The skulls were broken into from the rear and most probably, the brains served as food for true Homo sapiens. It would hardly be likely that the ancient ancestor of man lived concurrently with man and that his brains would be considered a delicacy of his great-grandchildren, homo sapiens. As early as 1957, French paleontologist, Dr. Marcellin Boule, proposed that the people who made the tools that killed Peking Man were true Homo sapiens.[53]

JAVA MAN

Dr. Eugene Dubois discovered another creature in the "Homo erectus" category, which he called "Java Man". Java Man was a skullcap and leg-bone. By the end of his life, Dubois recanted. He believed the leg-bone to belong to Homo sapiens and the skullcap that of a giant ape or gibbon.

HEIDELBERG MAN

The other commonly mentioned Homo erectus is Heidelberg Man. Johanson writes:

---

[52] Johanson and Maitland, p. 34.

[53] Marcellin Boule, *Fossil Men* (Dryden Press, 1957), p. 535.

"Heidelberg Man, for example, was named Homo heidelbergensis. His finder recognized that he was a man and, thus, belonged in the genus Homo, but decided to put him in a species of his own." [54]

Heidelberg Man consists of a single fossil -- a lower jaw with teeth.[55]   Heidelberg Man is imagination built around a "jawbone"!

"LUCY" AND THE AUSTRALOPITHECINES

Even Australopithecus is open to question. The star of this "human ancestor" is Donald Johanson's 3½ foot tall "Lucy". Supposedly, Lucy was the first creature to walk on two feet instead of four feet, like other apes did (and still do). Lucy resembles Homo sapiens in three ways (theoretically): her knee, arm-leg length, and left pelvic bone. She has a human-like knee joint, but this joint was found sixty to eighty meters deeper in the rock strata and almost a <u>mile</u> away from the rest of the skeleton. To claim that this knee joint belonged to a partial skeleton found about a mile away is as logical as saying a chicken drum stick bone found in the parking lot of the local Kentucky Fried Chicken establishment was originally the leg of a chicken whose partial skeleton was found in your back yard. There is no way to prove the knee-joint is part of Lucy's skeleton. Johanson published Lucy's arm-leg length ratio to be 83.9%. In other words her arm bone was said to be 83.9% as long as her leg bone. This would place her about midway between ape (arm and leg of equal length) and human (arm about 75% of leg length). The 83.9% seems quite specific, but the leg-bone had been broken in two or more places and one end was crushed. The pieces do not fit perfectly together, so

---

[54] Johanson, p. 36.

[55] Raymond, p. 280.

there is no way to accurately measure it. The 83.9% sounds good, but it is a guess (see Ex Nihilo, Vol. 6, 1983, p. 5).

The other human-like bone is the left pelvic bone. This bone is complete and is used to prove Lucy walked upright. The problem is that this bone does not prove upright walking. Johanson believes the bone has been distorted by some means. And yet, there is no other pelvic bone with which to compare it. The bone as it stands, more likely shows Lucy to have walked on all fours!

According to another evolutionist, Dr. Solly Zuckerman, Australopithecus is an ape and walked on all fours like an ape. Zuckerman evaluated the pelvic bone of the Australopithecines and he concluded that this telltale bone corresponded in one type of measurement to monkeys and baboons. Looking at it from another angle, it was "...completely unlike man, and identical with monkeys and apes.[56]

Fellow evolutionist Dr. Charles Oxnard, believes Australopithecus walked in a fashion similar to a chimpanzee[57] or an orangutan. Oxnard writes:

> "Let us now return to our original problem: the Australopithecine fossils. I shall not burden you with details of each and every study that we have made but...the information...shows that whereas the conventional wisdom is that the Australopithecine fragments are generally rather similar to humans and when different deviate somewhat towards the

---

[56] "It turned out that the angle of twist between the main plane of the ilium and the ischio-pubic part of the innominate in the Australopithecine cast corresponded to that in the four-footed macaque or cercopitheque monkeys and baboons,....Another dimension we have examined describes the length of the body of the ischium relative to the innominate as a whole...In this feature, Australopithecus is completely unlike man, and identical with monkeys and apes." Sir Solly Zuckerman, *Beyond the Ivory Tower* (New York: Taplinger Pub. Co., 1970), pp. 89,91.

[57] Dr. Chas. Oxnard, "Human Fossils: New Views of Old Bones," *American Biology Teacher*, Vol. 41, No. 5 (May, 1979), 264.

condition in African apes, the new studies point to different conclusions. The new investigations suggest that the fossil fragments are usually uniquely different from any living form; when they do have similarities with living species, they are as often as not reminiscent of the orangutan." [58]

Lyall Watson is right. There does not appear to be enough bones from "true" fossil man, "...to fill a single coffin."

ANTHROPOLOGICAL ART

Even the artwork typically used to depict these creatures is questionable. Those National Geographic-type pictures of apes gradually becoming more and more human until you finally see the man on the street (usually with an ape-like haircut and a beard) are called anthropological art.

"Unfortunately, the vast majority of artists' conceptions are based more on imagination, than evidence.... Much of the reconstruction, however, is guesswork. Bones say nothing about the fleshy parts of the nose, lips or ears. Artists must create something between an ape and a human being: the older a specimen is said to be, the more ape-like they make it.... Hairiness is a matter of pure conjecture.

The guesswork approach often leads to errors." [59]

How did the above words get into an evolutionary magazine like Science Digest? Those National Geographic pictures of "evolving" man are "artists' conceptions", "imagination", and "guesswork". When is the last time you saw a bone with hair on it? Or how do the artists know what kind of ears or lips to put on skull fragments or even whole

---

[58] Ibid, p. 273.

[59] Author unknown, "Anthropological Art," *Science Digest*, 89 No. 3 (April, 1981), 44.

skulls? There are no lips on skull bones. As <u>Science Digest</u> confesses, it is the artists' imagination. This is <u>not</u> science!

Every bone or bone particle discovered so far has been classified, by one evolution expert or another, as ape, monkey, or man -- not ape-man or man-ape.

IS A MONKEY ALMOST A MAN?

There are other facts to be considered when attempting to prove that man had ape-like evolutionary ancestors. J. W. Klotz lists a few of the important differences between man and the primates.[60] I have edited Dr. Klotz's list of 31 major differences down to the ten most outstanding in my opinion. If man evolved from the primates, then everything in the right column (characteristics of primates) would have to somehow evolve into the characteristics of man in the left column.

---

[60] J. W. Klotz, *Genes, Genesis, and Evolution* (St. Louis: Concordia Publishing House, 1972), pp. 332-336.

MAN	PRIMATE
1. Permanent bipedal locomotion	1. Walks on all fours
2. Great toe in line with other toes	2. Great toe like a thumb
3. Brain larger	3. Brain smaller
4. Head balanced on top of the spinal column	4. Head hinged in front of spinal column
5. Less mature at birth	5. More mature at birth
6. More vertebrae	6. Less vertebrae
7. Shorter arms	7. Longer arms
8. Longer legs	8. Shorter legs
9. One type hand	9. Another type hand
10. 46 chromosomes	10. 48 chromosomes

These are real, basic differences between man and the primates. Let us examine three.

THE GREAT TOE

What would it take to evolve a great toe like that on the foot of a primate into a great toe like that on the foot of a man? This digit on a primate is located and functions like a thumb. With its thumb-like great toe, it can grab onto a tree limb.

And yet the great toe of man comes out the front of his foot in a line with his other toes. In reality, there is no animal in the supposed evolutionary family of man with a great toe positioned somewhere between man's "out the front" and primate's "more toward the rear and out the side". There are no living animals and no fossil animals that display a great toe migrating toward the front of the foot. Surely "survival of the fittest" would ensnare and destroy any primate that lost its ability to grab limbs with its "evolving higher" great toe! It would quickly become extinct and would not evolve on up in the "evolutionary chain" to man.

HEAD PLACEMENT

The placement of the head is also quite significant. A human head is balanced on top of the spinal column to facilitate walking and running in the upright, two-legged position. Where is the evidence that the primates somehow managed to move their heads from being hinged in front of the spinal column (for ease of function on all fours) to the top of the spinal column as in humans? How could a creature function, whose head was placed halfway between the primate and man? Obviously, the "survival of the fittest" would catch up with it also. It would probably become extinct in one generation.

BABY HUMANS ARE HELPLESS

Evolution seems to be going in reverse as you look at the ability of human babies to survive, compared to the primates. Human babies are totally helpless at birth and for months afterward. Baby apes are ready to run to safety or climb onto their mother's back for a ride soon after birth. How would those first human babies have survived? And, what is the probability that the last set of ape-parents would give birth to dizygotic twins (a male and female) which could not only survive as the first non-ape human babies, but could reproduce offspring (male and female) which could again reproduce and on and on? And, why do we still have so many species of apes and monkeys, if they are evolving into something else, perhaps even into people? Again may I emphasize the fact that what we see in real life today and over the span of recorded history are discrete, identifiable animals, plants and people; not intermediate, transitional life forms.

A MASSIVE POPULATION PROBLEM

If, as evolutionists believe, monkey-like creatures evolved into man about 1 million years ago, (Lucy is said to be around 2.8 million years old), we would anticipate a massive population problem. Dr. Henry Morris gives some interesting figures in his book, Biblical Cosmology and Modern Science, published in 1970. Assuming parents lived to the age of 35 and had four children, roughly 3 billion people would have been produced in just the first thousand years! You might say, "Well, that is too many children." Dr. Morris shows the figures for a family with three children, using the same condition as above. In roughly 2 thousand years the population of earth would have reached about 4 1/2 billion. With 2.5 children per family and extending the length of a generation to 43 years, in little more than 4 thousand years 3 billion people would populate the earth. To quote Dr. Morris verbatim: "It begins to be glaringly evident that the human race cannot be very old!" [61]

According to Dr. Morris, if the earth's population started with two people 4,300 years ago, it would only have to increase at the rate of 0.5% per year in order to reach the population of the world of 1970. This 0.5% is significantly less than the 1970 population growth rate of about 2% per year. The farther back in history you go, the higher is the percentage of growth. Less industrialized people have bigger families on the average.

Dr. Morris states that the best secular estimate of world population at the time of Christ, is 200,000,000 people. Using 2.75 children per family, plus a 40-year generation and starting with 2 people in 2340 B.C., there would have been

---

[61] Henry M. Morris, *Biblical Cosmology and Modern Science* (Nutley, New Jersey: Craig Press, 1970), p. 75.

about 210 million people alive in A.D. 1. These figures would fit the Biblical time frame nicely.

Bringing into consideration the effects of disease and wars on population growth, Dr. Morris says:

> "But what about the possibility that the great plagues and wars of the past may have served to keep the population from growing at the indicated rates? Could the population have remained static for long ages and only in modern times have started to expand?
>
> We are unable to answer these questions dogmatically, of course, since population data are unavailable for earlier times....
>
> Furthermore, there is really no evidence that the growth of population has been retarded by wars or disease epidemics. The past century, which has experienced the greatest mushrooming of populations, has also witnessed the most destructive wars in all history, as well as the worst plagues and famines." [62]

Dr. Morris singles out the Jewish people as a good example of the accuracy of his population estimates. The Jewish people had no homeland for many years. They suffered persecution and the holocaust. Morris states that if the average Jewish family had 2.4 children and a 43-year generation, that in 3,700 years (beginning about the time of the patriarch, Jacob) there should have been 13,900,000 Jewish people alive by 1970. [63]

Man could not possibly have been here as man for even 1,000,000 years. Using Morris' figures, 1,000,000 years is over 28,600 generations, which would put the world population of 1970 at 10 to the 5,000th power! That is enough people to fill the entire universe, and we are not including rats and rabbits. As Dr. Morris said,

---

[62] Ibid, p. 76.

[63] Ibid, p. 77.

"It begins to be glaringly evident that the human race cannot be very old! ...the assumption of the evolutionists that man first appeared a million or more years ago becomes completely absurd when examined in the light of population statistics." [64]

If man has been recognizable as man for 30 million years, 15 million years or even 500,000 years, there should be hundreds of billions of fossils scattered in huge piles all over the earth! Where is fossil man? Let's face it -- man has not been and cannot have been on earth for very much longer than a few thousand years! If studies of population statistics demand a short (few thousand years) history of man on earth, then evolution of man over thousands or millions of years is, most unlikely if not totally, impossible!

PREHISTORIC MAN IS NOT PREHISTORIC

Could it be that "prehistoric" man was not "before history" after all? Job may have been referring to the type of people scientists call "cavemen" as he wrote:

"But now they that are younger than I have me in derision, whose fathers I would have disdained to have set with the dogs of my flock.
Yea, whereto might the strength of their hands *profit* me, in whom old age was perished?
For want and famine they were solitary; fleeing into the wilderness in former time desolate and waste.
Who cut up mallows by the bushes, and juniper roots *for* their meat.
They were driven forth from among men, (they cried after them as after a thief;)
To dwell in the cliffs of the valleys, *in* caves of the earth, and in the rocks.

---

[64] Ibid, pp. 75, 77.

> **Among the bushes they brayed; under the nettles they were gathered together.**
> **They were children of fools, yea, children of base men: they were viler than the earth." (Job 30:l-8)**

Perhaps "cavemen" were cast-offs from the civilized societies of their day. Possibly these were people given over to a reprobate mind due to their habitual sin and decadence. In any event, they were not man's ancestors. They lived concurrently with man.

The God of the Bible says He created man after His own image from the dust of the earth:

> **"And the Lord God formed man of the dust from the ground, and breathed into his nostrils the breath of life; and man became a living soul." (Genesis 2:7)**

God formed man from dust, not from some prehistoric, ape-like, hominid creature or the primordial ooze. The dust became, by God's creative design and power, a man; but the man had no life until God breathed life into him. Genesis 2:7 clearly shows that man's emergence from some previous living creature is not true. He came from non-living dust which became, by God's creative design and power, a man -- a man which had no life until the living God breathed life into him. This means that man could not have evolved from some more primitive "LIVING" monkey-like creature. People were created by God in God's own image. There can be no compromise for the Christian as to the origin of man. We did not come from monkey-like creatures but through the indescribable, unfathomable, supernatural power of the God of the Bible.

THE ANTHROPIC PRINCIPLE

God placed man, the pinnacle of His creation, in a special environment of delicately balanced systems. Scientists are now calling this balance of ecosystems (that support the life of man) the "Anthropic Principle". For our lives to be maintained we must have exactly the correct amounts of oxygen, hydrogen, carbon dioxide, sunlight, magnetic field, speed of rotation and revolution of earth, distance from the moon, distance from the sun, ozone, water, gravity, etc., etc., etc. All of these factors must be in the correct amounts, in the right places, at the right times, and in exact relationships with each other. For instance, if our earth's gravity was weaker, our atmosphere would thin out and be unable to support life. If gravity was stronger, undesirable gases such as ammonia gas would be held in higher concentrations and be detrimental to life. That means our earth has to have been made exactly the right size to generate the perfect amount of gravity to support our atmosphere. But it also had to be the right size to hold our moon in orbit -- that means the moon had to be made the right size so it wouldn't drift off into space or crash into earth -- and the moon also had to be the right size so that the ocean tides stay under control. We could go on and on with this, but the fact is the evolution model as an explanation for this incredible universe comes up grossly lacking! God, the God of the Bible, is to be praised and He, alone, is to receive the glory and the honor. **"It is a good thing to give thanks to the Lord and to sing praises unto thy name, O most High." (Psalm 92:1)**

MARVEL OF GOD'S CREATION #5
The Giraffe

Let us look at another of the marvels of God's creation -- the giraffe. The giraffe had to be created as a fully, functional and unique animal.[65] A mature bull giraffe grows to be about 18 feet tall. In order to pump blood up his long neck to his brain, the giraffe needs a powerful pump. His heart is about 2½ feet long. It is so powerful that, as the animal bends down to satisfy its thirst, the blood pressure is more than enough to burst the blood vessels of the brain.

Evolution says something does not evolve until it is needed. But the giraffe would not know it needed to protect its brain from the devastation of excessive blood pressure until it had died of brain hemorrhage while taking a cool drink. How can it "evolve" a protective mechanism, after it knows it needs it, if it is no longer alive to do it?

The giraffe has a protective mechanism which was designed by our Creator. As the bull bends his head down for a drink, valves in the arteries in its neck begin to close. Blood beyond the last valve continues moving toward the brain. But instead of passing at high speed and pressing into the brain and damaging or destroying it, that last pump is shunted under the brain into a group of vessels similar to a sponge. The brain is preserved and the powerful surge of oxygenated blood gently expands this "sponge" beneath it.

---

[65] *God in Creation* by Bob Devine, Chicago: Moody Press, 1982, pp. 35-37 describes the giraffe and the necessity of a Creator. This booklet shows how ten different animals and plants demand a Creator by their special features.

However, from this mechanism another problem arises. A lion creeps up and prepares to kill its spotted prey. The giraffe quickly raises its head and, without something to compensate for the reduced blood flow, passes out. It got up too fast for the low pressure and oxygen content of the brain. The lion eats a hearty meal and the giraffe were it alive, would realize that it had better evolve some mechanism to re-oxygenate its oxygen-deprived brain! We all know that dead animals don't evolve anything, even though evolution demands its creatures realize they need an improvement before that improvement begins to evolve.

But the giraffe survives! The Creator designed it in such a way that as he begins to raise his head, the arterial valves open. The "sponge" squeezes its oxygenated blood into the brain, the veins going down the neck contain some valves which close to help level out the blood pressure, and the giraffe can quickly be erect and running without passing out and becoming lion lunch. God made the giraffe just like it is with all systems complete and ready for any emergency. There is no way the giraffe could have evolved its special features. The functional mechanisms of the giraffe demand God to be their Creator. Why not God as the Creator of everything?

Everyone agrees -- a giraffe is a giraffe. It is a distinct species, a discrete entity. No one would say a giraffe is a "missing link" or a "transitional form". A giraffe is not some creature emerging from some other creature or changing into a "higher" or more complex animal -- a giraffe is a giraffe! It can be scientifically examined with results that display the necessity of a single creative act. This long-necked creature had to have been originally formed with all of its complex features fully functional.

The giraffe testifies to the existence of its Creator!

6

THE
TEN COMMANDMENTS
AND THE DAYS OF THE
CREATION WEEK

In 1971, two students had the courage to politely challenge one of their professors (me) to defend his position on the origin of all things. That seemed to be a fairly easy job since I was convinced that huge volumes of factual scientific evidence proved evolution (over billions of years) to be true. By 1972, this professor's stomach was churning with frustration! The evidence for an old universe promoted as proven fact by evolutionists was nowhere to be found. This is not to say that there is lack of writing on the subject of evolution, but that there is no true scientific evidence that is not based on assumptions (refer back to the beginning of Chapter 2, "seven basic assumptions").

It was obvious to me back in the early 70's that evolution needed long periods of time. Couldn't those days of Genesis 1 be a billion years each? If we can somehow impose long periods of time onto the text of Genesis 1, evolution and the Bible quite nicely harmonize with each other. Or so I thought.

24-HOUR DAYS OR AEONS OF TIME?

Those days of Genesis are 24-hour days! If we believe the Bible, they cannot be one billion years each. Even the logic in the Ten Commandments demands 24-hour days [It wouldn't hurt any of us to review the Ten Commandments], so let's make some observations from Exodus 20:1-20:

1. **And God spake all these words, saying,**
2. **I am the Lord thy God, which have brought thee out of the land of Egypt, out of the house of bondage.**
3. **Thou shalt have no other gods before me.**
4. **Thou shalt not make unto thee any graven image, or any likeness of any thing that is in heaven above, or that is in the earth beneath, or that is in the water under the earth:**
5. **Thou shalt not bow down thyself to them, nor serve them: for I the Lord thy God am a jealous God, visiting the iniquity of the fathers upon the children unto the third and fourth generation of them that hate me;**
6. **And showing mercy unto thousands of them that love me, and keep my commandments.**
7. **Thou shalt not take the name of the Lord thy God in vain; for the Lord will not hold him guiltless that taketh his name in vain.**
8. **Remember the sabbath day, to keep it holy.**
9. **Six days shalt thou labour, and do all thy work:**
10. **But the seventh day is the sabbath of the Lord thy God: in it thou shalt not do any work, thou, nor thy son, nor thy**

daughter, thy manservant, nor thy maidservant, nor thy cattle, nor thy stranger that is within thy gates:

11. For in six days, the Lord made heaven and earth, the sea, and all that in them is, and rested the seventh day: wherefore the Lord blessed the sabbath day, and hallowed it.

12. Honour thy father and thy mother: that thy days may be long upon the land which the Lord thy God giveth thee.

13. Thou shalt not kill.

14. Thou shalt not commit adultery.

15. Thou shalt not steal.

16. Thou shalt not bear false witness against thy neighbor.

17. Thou shalt not covet thy neighbour's house, thou shalt not covet thy neighbour's wife, nor his manservant, nor his maidservant, nor his ox, nor his ass, nor any thing that is thy neighbour's.

18. And all the people saw the thunderings, and the lightnings, and the noise of the trumpet, and the mountain smoking: and when the people saw it, they removed, and stood afar off.

19. And they said unto Moses, Speak thou with us, and we will hear: but let not God speak with us, lest we die.

20. And Moses said unto the people, Fear not: for God is come to prove you, and that his fear may be before your faces, that ye sin not.

Did you notice that man's work week is parallel to God's work week (Exodus 20:9-11)? Thus, if man works six 24-hour days, then the logic of Exodus 20:11 requires that God worked six 24-hour days and rested during the seventh day as man is to rest one day a week.

Hebrew scholars universally agree that the days (the Hebrew word "yom") of Genesis 1, are 24-hour days. These scholars may not necessarily believe that God has the ability to create everything in six normal days, or they may not even believe that the Bible is God's inspired Word, but they do believe the Hebrew word, yom, means 24-hour day. Liberal scholars have tried to claim that some primitive writer who had no knowledge of science and geology wrote down a brief account of the origin of man in overly simplistic terms.

Many scholars say that it does not matter what the words say, but simply that it is the meaning or the message behind these "word-symbols" that is important. However, if that is true, then we might as well throw out the Hebrew and Greek lexicons (dictionaries). Every word in Genesis 1, is in the Hebrew lexicon. Every word has a definite meaning and we can look up what that meaning is. It is not some nebulous "word-symbol" that is limited in meaning only by the extent of the imagination of the reader.

More than ninety-eight percent of the time that yom (day) is used in the Old Testament (over 2,500 times), it means 24-hour day or the daylight part of a standard day. The rest of the time it refers to such things as the "Day of the Lord", which scholars argue could be anywhere from a 24-hour day to 1,000 plus years to eternity. The fact is that Genesis 1, uses yom with clarifiers such as day one, day two, etc. Everywhere else in the Bible that yom is used with clarifiers (numbers one, two, three, etc.) it unquestionably indicates a 24-hour day.

EACH DAY IS HALF LIGHT AND HALF DARK

God used every word He possibly could to show us He is referring to one rotation of the earth in front of its source of light or 24-hour "yoms" in Genesis 1. He literally says, "...There was evening and there was morning, day one; ...there was evening and there was morning, day two"; etc. Each day had an evening and each day had a morning. In Genesis 1:5, God says, **"And God called the light Day (yom), and the darkness He called Night.   And the evening and the morning were the first day."**

Notice that each day was part light and part darkness. This eliminates theistic evolution and day-age theories, since each day (one billion years?) would be half light and half dark! You cannot evolve anything in 500 million years of darkness or, for that matter, in 500 million-year stretches of unrelenting sunlight.

We might ask, "How old was Adam when he died?" Genesis 5:5 reads: **"And all the days that Adam lived were nine hundred and thirty years: and he died."** If one single Genesis 1 day equals one billion years as evolution demands, and Adam lived through at least half of day six, all of day seven and 930 more years, then how old was Adam when he died? Was he, let's say, 1 billion 500 million 930 years old? Or did he die at the age of 930? You can't have both! You can't have long periods of time (day-age, theistic evolution, progressive creation) and the Bible. Either Adam was 930 years old when he died, or you can throw out Genesis 1:1 through 5:5!!

DAYS, YEARS AND SEASONS

God had words that He could have used if He had wanted us to understand those days of Genesis, Chapter 1, to be longer than 24 hours. One of these Hebrew words is "olam". Olam means a long period of time and can even mean everlasting. God put all the necessary words into the Hebrew text to make it unmistakably clear to the reader -- these are 24-hour days.

Look at Genesis 1:14:

"And God said, Let there be lights in the firmament of the heaven to divide the day from the night; and let them be for signs, and for seasons, and for days, and years".

God here differentiates between days and seasons and years. How can anyone stretch a Genesis 1 day into a billion years and then make any sense at all of Genesis 1:14? If a day is a billion years, then how long is a season or a year? Is a Biblical year 365 billion years? Even the most radical evolutionists claim the universe is not much older than twenty-billion years! God lines up all these time words for us in one verse to prove that He means 24-hour days. You can't make any sense at all of Genesis 1:14, if you insist on the theistic evolution or day-age or progressive creation views. (Don't forget -- we do not subject the Bible to science, we subject science to the Bible.) If "science" tells us we must have long geologic ages to explain the existence of all things, but the Bible says God did it all in six normal days, then we must believe the Bible by faith and know that science has some more research to do to catch up with the Bible.

The Ten Commandments in the Bible are one of the root causes of belief in the evolution model. Scientifically credentialed people closely examine God's creation. What they see is the handiwork of God (Romans 1 and Psalm 19), but they nevertheless choose to believe the lie of evolution because they do not want to acknowledge their sin, as recorded in the Ten Commandments. To accept belief in God, who wrote those Ten Commandments with His own finger, becomes unthinkable. Belief would place man in a position of submission and obedience to his Creator. Furthermore, this position of submission and obedience demands responsibility before this holy God and ultimately, the certainty of judgment -- realities that people do not like to think about. We know we are sinners. We cannot even live up to our own standards, let alone God's righteous standards. It is easier to live in the fantasy-land of evolution than in reality when we are separated from our Creator by our own unholiness and pride. Life appears to be less complicated and more comfortable as we believe the lie of evolution.

No rational person would argue that God's Ten Commandments are invalid or inaccurate or harmful to society. If obeyed by everyone, we would have a near-perfect, crime-free and pollution-free world.

Did you notice that the seven-day creation week is mentioned in the Ten Commandments (Exodus 20:11)? Is this not fascinating? In view of all the many things the Creator could have mentioned to be preserved forever, He chose, in the midst of His Ten Commandments, to call attention to the original seven-day week of creation.

There is no question about the English translation of the Ten Commandments. What we read is precisely what God said. He said, **"For in six days the Lord made heaven and earth, the sea and all that in them is..."** (Exodus 20:11) That means exactly what it says. In a literal six days, the Lord made everything that exists, whether it exists in the heavens or on the earth or in the seas. He made it <u>functionally mature</u> and <u>with the appearance of age</u>. That would include the entirety of the macrouniverse (stars, planets, sun, moon, comets, asteroids, angels, etc.) and the microuniverse (the molecules, atoms and quarks, of elephants, beetles and sharks). A six-day creation leaves no room at all for theistic evolution and its billions of years, or for a "gap" between Genesis 1:1 and 1:2. Some of the early twentieth century Bible scholars came to believe in a "gap theory" due to the influence of evolutionary "science". These godly men believed that science had established great geologic ages and "prehistoric" man to be a proven fact. They went to the early Chapters of Genesis and attempted to subject the Bible to science by postulating a "gap" between Genesis 1:1 and 1:2.   But the sun, stars, heat, light, atmosphere and universe were not yet created. Nothing existed nor could it exist in the supposed "gap" between Genesis 1:1 and 1:2. There was no "pre-Adamic" race of wicked people living in the "gap". Not only could they have not existed without light, but sin and wickedness did not enter the universe until the fall of Adam.

Romans 5:12 teaches:

"Wherefore, as by one man (Adam) sin entered into the world, and death by sin; and so death passed upon all men, for that all have sinned."

A sobering result of Adam's sin was death, but before Adam's sin there was <u>no</u> death. If there was no death before Adam (the very clear statement of God's word), then it would be impossible to have "pre-Adamic" people dying.

Actually, the entire creation was affected by Adam's sin and it still "groans" with thorns, thistles and entropy as it awaits its redemption. Romans 8:22-23 states:

"For we know that the whole creation groaneth and travaileth in pain together until now.
And not only they, but ourselves also, which have the firstfruits of the Spirit, even we ourselves groan within ourselves, waiting for the adoption, to wit, the redemption of our body."

Holding to the "gap" position not only demands death before the Fall, but it also forces changes in the Biblical text. Genesis 1:2 must be changed from **"And the earth <u>was</u> without form and void"** to "and the earth <u>became</u> without form and void." God uses the very same word for "was" in Genesis 2:25 and 3:1. Genesis 2:25 says: **"And they <u>were</u> both naked..."** Adam and Eve were not created with clothes and then "became" naked. The same can be said for the serpent in 3:1. It is not that he "became" crafty after not being crafty; he <u>was</u> crafty from the beginning. The Gap theory necessitates changes in other Biblical texts also. For a comprehensive study of problems with the Gap theory please read Dr. John Whitcomb's book <u>The Early Earth: Revised</u>

Edition. We do not need to accommodate Scripture to what we might believe to be factual science -- the geological ages -- by imposing a gap between Genesis 1:1 and 1:2 or by stretching the 24-hour days of Genesis 1 into long ages of geologic time. Men who have done this, most probably in all innocence, violate a basic rule: The Bible must never be subjected to science, but science must always be subjected to the Bible.

My position, quite frankly, is of one who committed his life to the Lord Jesus Christ later in life than most (age 27) and who endured a gut-wrenching five-year struggle with this issue. When I came to faith in Jesus Christ as my Lord and Savior, I became a theistic evolutionist. I then saw, as many men and women have seen (when exposed to the true truth of the Bible), the total "rightness" and reality of God's six-day creation. The science I studied showed the incredible complexity of every plant, animal and insect and yet had no sane answer to the "why" and "how" of this complexity except to say, "no one plus nothing equals everything" or "all that 'is' results from the impersonal plus chance plus time." Our God, the Almighty Creator, does not need time. He is above time. The Creator, the Lord Jesus, displayed His supernatural ability to act without time restraints through His miracles. When we believe Genesis 1 as it is written, we bow in worship and in submissive trust of our awesome, infinite Creator. As Job said:

> "I know that Thou canst do every thing, and that no thought can be withholden from thee."
> "I have heard of thee by the hearing of the ear: but now my eye seeth thee."
> "Wherefore I abhor myself, and repent in dust and ashes."
> (Job 42:2, 5, 6)

Earlier, we mentioned (Scott Huse, The Collapse of Evolution, and Walter Brown, In the Beginning) the documentation showing that the details of evolution and the specifics of Genesis 1 do not match up. For example, evolution says reptiles developed first and then birds evolved out of reptiles, but the Bible says birds came first (Genesis 1:20-23) and then reptiles (Genesis 1:24-26). If we again go back to thinking about the days of Genesis, then certain things are not logical when we hold to long periods of time. For example, God made plants on the third day (Genesis 1:12, 13), but He created insects on the sixth day. Many plants need insects to pollinate them. How could they survive more than two billion years, while waiting for insects to "evolve"?

Evolutionary theory does not have the answers for how we got here. Evolution forces us to throw out the clearly written and easily understood words of Genesis 1-11, since the two are not compatible. Do we believe the Bible or have we placed our trust in the foolish speculations of men, based on the foundation of the scientifically unprovable assumptions of so-called science (see the beginning of Chapter 2, "seven basic assumptions")?

Since origins are scientifically unverifiable for either evolution or creation, then we are dealing with "faith". No human was there to verify the "Big Bang" and no person was there to witness the Creation.

Many of us easily profess to believe in Jesus Christ as the virgin-born Son of the one true God and in His resurrection from the dead. We accept this truth, without flinching, but we limit God to a "Trial and Error" entity not capable of "speaking the Creation into existence", but rather relying on billions of years and an evolutionary process to finally "get it right".

It is my contention that the main reason for rejecting a creationist view (especially in light of the statements by evolutionists which give the creationist position credence) is mankind's basic pride and rebellion. Evolution allows us to be independent of God so that we do not feel any accountability to God. Evolution takes some pressure off our conscience!

The current, pervasive New Age teaching that "we each have within ourselves the god consciousness and can achieve godhood by our own strength as we learn to look within ourselves and develop our full potential" further fans the flames of self-sufficiency, selfishness and independence from any power greater than ourselves. This New Age teaching promotes evolution and is deadly deception. It is the way of death as it leads people to reject the Lord Jesus Christ as their personal Savior. New Age evolutionary thinking also convinces people that they cannot believe the first eleven chapters of <u>Genesis</u> to be the <u>literal</u> Word of God.

FLOOD WATERS COVERED THE EARTH

Included early in Genesis is the account of Noah and the flood. If evolution is true, then a global flood taking place about 5 thousand years ago is impossible! Evolution demands millions of years, not just a few thousand, for creatures and ecosystems to evolve. We sometimes hear this historical event referred to as the flood of Noah. It was not Noah's flood. It was God's flood! The flood was God's judgment on the sin which had spread to cover the earth. Genesis 6:5-14a describes God's heartbreak at the sinfulness of mankind and His recognition of Noah as the only righteous man on the face of the earth.

"And God saw that the wickedness of man was great in the earth, and that every imagination of the thoughts of his heart was only evil continually.

And it repented the Lord that he had made man on the earth, and it grieved him in his heart.

And the Lord said, I will destroy man whom I have created from the face of the earth; both man,and beast, and the creeping thing, and the fowls of the air; for it repenteth me that I have made them.

But Noah found grace in the eyes of the Lord.

These are the generations of Noah: Noah was a just man, and perfect in his generations, and Noah walked with God.

And Noah begat three sons, Shem, Ham and Japheth.

The earth also was corrupt before God, and the earth was filled with violence.

And God looked upon the earth, and, behold, it was corrupt; for all flesh had corrupted his way upon the earth.

And God said to Noah, The end of all flesh is come before me; for the earth is filled with violence through them; and, behold, I will destroy them with the earth.

Make thee an ark of gopher wood...."

THE DESTRUCTION
OF ALL LAND-BASED FLESH

What has God told us was His purpose in sending the global flood? Genesis 6:5 records that God saw the great wickedness and evil in mankind. Genesis 6:17 states the actual purpose of the flood: **"... to destroy all flesh."** The types of life to be destroyed are more specifically listed in Genesis 7:21-23:

"And all flesh died that moved upon the earth, both of fowl, and of cattle, and of beast, and of every creeping thing that creepeth upon the earth, and every man:

All in whose nostrils was the breath of life, of all that was in the dry land, died.

And every living substance was destroyed which was upon the face of the ground, both man, and cattle, and the

**creeping things, and to fowl of the heaven; and they were
destroyed from the earth: and Noah only remained alive, and
they that were with him in the ark."**

The purpose of this great judgment by water was to destroy
all dry-land life. Dry-land life extended well beyond the
Tigris and Euphrates valley! The flood was not designed to
destroy marine life although many water creatures were
destroyed by the flood as is seen in the fossil record.

Peter tells us (II Peter 3:5-13) that there are three heaven
and earth systems in God's eternal plan. The first system was
totally destroyed by the water of the flood which was the
judgment of God in Noah's day. Remember it was the
violence (Gen. 6:11) that moved God to judgment! (What is
the content of the movies and cartoons that you and your
family are watching? Have you noticed the geometric
increases in violence?)

The second heaven and earth system (our present system,
II Peter 3:7) will be destroyed by fire so hot as to destroy
even the foundational molecules of the earth and sky (II
Peter 3:10). The root of sin, wickedness and violence will
finally be burned out of existence. So, how are you investing
your resources (time, money, talents)? Only three things will
not be burned up -- God; God's Word, the Bible; and people.
Are you investing eternally in God's Word and people?

The third heaven and earth system is called the new
heavens and new earth (II Peter 3:13). This eternal,
righteous heaven and earth system is also referred to in
Romans 8:21, Revelation 21:1 and perhaps Isaiah 65:17. It
will last forever. Only those whose names are written in the
Lamb's Book of Life will inherit the New Heavens and New
Earth. Have you come to the sacrificial Lamb, the Creator
Jesus, in faith believing that He alone has the power and right
to save your soul? Have you committed the rest of your life
to Him and to His service?

The Lord Jesus contrasted the days of Noah and the flood judgment to His Second Coming:

> **"And as it was in the days of Noah, so shall it be also in the days of the Son of man.**
> **They did eat, they drank, they married wives, they were given in marriage, until the day that Noah entered into the ark, and the flood came, and destroyed them all." (Luke 17:26, 27)**

The flood is treated in the Bible as an actual event. Noah is not some mythical character. The Lord Jesus and writers of the Bible believed and taught about a literal man named Noah and an actual global flood. Nowhere in the Bible is the flood characterized as a local river overflow as some scholars have hypothesized. The words of Genesis 6-9 have concrete meanings in the Hebrew lexicons. These are not symbols depicting a mythological event recorded by some primitive scribe whose concept of the world was limited to the banks of the Euphrates and Tigris Rivers. This flood covered **"...all the high hills that were under the whole heaven..." (Genesis 7:19 Emphasis added)**. The heaven here referred to is the atmospheric heavens surrounding our earth where the birds fly (see Genesis 1:20).

THE ARK OF NOAH

Would God move Noah to build an ark 437 feet long, 73 feet wide and 44 feet deep for a local river overflow? The ark was big enough to carry, on one deck, all the kinds of dry land animals needed to repopulate the earth. Scientists have estimated that Noah would have to take about 35,000 sheep-sized animals on the ark to give us all the kinds of creatures we have today. The ark was big enough to carry 125,000 sheep-sized animals. 35,000 creatures could have been kept on one of the three floors in the ark. Noah probably took young animals (even baby dinosaurs) since they would eat less and take up less space. Noah and his family could have lived on the top deck and he could have trapped the insects on the bottom deck.

Would you need an ark to save birds during a local river overflow? Have you ever heard of a local river overflow that lasted longer than a year? The Genesis flood did.[66] Why would God give Noah 120 years to build the ark (Genesis 6:3) when it would have been much easier to move his family and flocks out of the Mesopotamian Valley? In 120 years Noah could have moved quite a distance away from the flood if it was just a local river overflow! Dr. John Morris has an excellent video on this very subject called The Deluge, filmed on location at Mt. Ararat in Turkey. It is produced by I.C.R., P.O. Box 2667 El Cajon, CA   92021, (619) 448-0900.

Could God have taken care of Noah, his family and that ark-load of creatures for a whole year? Genesis 8:1 begins by saying: **"And God remembered Noah, and every living thing, and all the cattle that was with him...."** That word "remembered" is a special word. It has the idea in the text of the Hebrew language of intimate care and watchfulness. The concept of knowing needs and acting on that knowledge is contained in the word. It was not that Noah was stranded in the ark and God had been busy doing other things. Then God suddenly looked down and said, "Oh, my! I just remembered Noah." This word carries with it the concept of meeting needs.

Some creationists have posited that the process of hibernation may have begun during the flood. Perhaps many

---

[66] For much more information about the Flood-judgment of God read: *The Genesis Flood* by Henry Morris and John Whitcomb (Philadelphia: The Presbyterian & Reformed Pub. Co., 1961).

animals slept through most of the ride. Numerous animals that do not normally hibernate can be made to do so in certain laboratory conditions. The ability to hibernate is displayed by such animals as: bats, skunks, woodchucks, prairie dogs, badgers, bears, certain mice, humming birds, garter snakes, turtles, toads, spiders, beetles, dragonflies, grasshoppers, garden snails, etc. etc. It is not impossible to believe that some, if not many, animals slept a good part of that year. Many Bible "scoffers" refer to Noah and the Ark as just a myth or story and not an actual historical event. This could be, in part, because of the seeming impossibility of so few people caring for that large a number of animals. Hibernation of the animals and insects would definitely have decreased the time demands for feeding and scooping by the eight human ark passengers. No one can say exactly what went on in the sealed ark, but God knew and cared and saw to it that the remnant of His creatures survived.

THE ALTAR, THE RAINBOW AND THE DRUNKENNESS

Remember what happened when Noah came out of the ark? Three major things come to mind: the altar, the rainbow and the drunkenness. The first recorded event in the life of Noah after his departure from the ark was his worship. He built an altar to the Lord and worshipped His Savior. Genesis 8:20-21:

> "And Noah builded an altar unto the Lord; and took of every clean beast, and of every clean fowl, and offered burnt offerings on the altar.
>
> And the Lord smelled a sweet savour; and the Lord said in his heart, I will not again curse the ground any more for man's sake; for the imagination of man's heart is evil from his youth; neither will I again smite any more every thing living, as I have done."

As a result, God gave Noah the promise of the rainbow. Was the rainbow God's Covenantal sign to man that He would never again send a local river overflow? Of course not! If it was a local river overflow in the known "world" of the writer's day, then the rainbow as a covenantal sign means nothing. There have been many local river overflows in the Middle East since Noah's day. The rainbow means God will never again destroy life upon the earth with a flood.

The account of Noah's drunkenness is also important in the study of creationism. There may be several reasons for the inclusion of this episode in God's eternal Word, but it could very readily serve as a hint that man is no longer living in heaven and earth system #1 now that the flood is over. The pre-flood environmental and ecological system (#1) was destroyed by the flood. The present heaven and earth system (#2) is different.

Reading certain selections from II Peter 3 presents to the reader God's eternal plan, which includes three heaven and earth systems: The heaven and earth of Adam and Noah (system #1); the present heaven and earth (system #2); and the New Heavens and new Earth of eternity (system #3).

3.   Knowing this first, that there shall come in the last days scoffers, walking after their own lusts,

4.   And saying, Where is the promise of his coming? for since the fathers fell asleep, all things continue as they were from the beginning of the creation.

5.   For this they willingly are ignorant of, that by the word of God the heavens were of old, and the earth standing out of the water and in the water:

6.   Whereby the world that then was, being overflowed with water, perished:

7.   But the heavens and the earth, which are now, by the same word are kept in store, reserved unto fire against the day of judgment and perdition of ungodly men.

10.   But the day of the Lord will come as a thief in the night; in the which the heavens shall pass away with a great noise,

**and the elements shall melt with fervent heat, the earth also
and the works that are therein shall be burned up.
13. Nevertheless we, according to his promise, look for new
heavens and a new earth, wherein dwelleth righteousness. (II
Peter 3 selections)**

It is probable that heaven and earth system #1 had a
heavier atmosphere than our present system (#2).   The
increased atmospheric pressure was the result of God taking
water off the surface of the earth (see Genesis 1:6-8) and
putting it above atmospheric heaven or, more specifically,
the expanse or firmament that the birds fly in (see Genesis
1:20). These "waters above" came down in Noah's day and
may have set up the condition that quite possibly caused
Noah's drunkenness.

Alcohol ferments faster and gets into your blood and
brain more quickly in system #2 than it did in system #1
because the atmospheric pressure was reduced by at least one
half as the water came down as rain. Alcohol fermentation
rates are doubled when the pressure is cut in half. It appears
that Noah was caught by surprise. He was God's righteous
man. He had not forgotten to make an altar and sacrifice in
worship of his Lord and Savior. Noah probably made the
same amount of wine that he made before the flood. But
now, in system #2 with the atmospheric pressure less than
one half of what it was in system #1 when Noah entered the
ark, the wine would ferment at least twice as fast and get into
his physical system twice as fast -- catching Noah with a
surprise inebriation. We have no record that Noah ever got
drunk before or after this incident. Perhaps one reason our
Creator gives us this sad account is to hint at the difference
between system #1 and system #2.

Our present heaven and earth are vastly different than the
pre-flood heaven and earth of Noah's day. That is the reason
we do not have dragon flies with a wingspread of 32 inches,

or chambered nautilus shells eight feet tall or 300,000 pound dinosaurs walking the earth today. And yet people lived in system #1 and are still thriving in system #2. Only God could have designed life to work efficiently in two significantly different systems. There is no one like Him!

6.   Forasmuch as there is none like unto thee, O Lord; thou art great, and thy name is great in might.
12. He hath made the earth by his power, he hath established the world by his wisdom, and hath stretched out the heavens by his discretion.
16. The Lord of hosts is his name. (Jeremiah 10:6,12,16)

MARVEL OF GOD'S CREATION #6
The Angler Fish

One of God's amazing creations is the deep-sea Angler fish. This fish makes its home more than a mile deep in ocean water. On her forehead the female has a "fishing rod" tipped with an "artificial worm". She dangles this "bait" over her mouth to attract her next meal. Ah, but there is a problem -- her next meal cannot see the bait, since it is too dark under more than a mile of sea water. Starvation sets in while she waits for her first deep sea fish dinner. At last, she realizes "I must do something about this darkness problem". But, alas, it is too late. She is dead and dead fish can not evolve the adaptations needed to rectify problems, even though evolution says she doesn't evolve something until her situation (or environment) tells her that it is needed to survive.

The only possibility is that God created the Angler fish with all the fully-functional equipment it needed to survive at great depths. To solve the darkness problem, God created a special kind of light on the bait. This light displays highly advanced technology -- it gives off no heat! A compound called Luciferin is oxidized with the help of an enzyme scientists named Luciferase, and this reaction produces heatless light. Ask an evolutionist how a deep-sea fish could evolve the ability to produce high-tech light on an artificial bait dangled over the fish's mouth? God has made His creation to display His glory and power. No one could look at the Angler fish and say it is the result of the "impersonal plus time plus chance", unless that person had already decided to refuse to believe in the God of the Bible (Romans

1). The vain speculations of evolution lead to foolish thinking and impossible conclusions.

Naturally, the Angler fish needs to reproduce and has a special way of doing this. In the darkness of the deep, it is difficult for the male and female to find each other. God designed the eggs of the female so that they float up through a mile of ocean to the surface. On the ocean surface the eggs form a jellylike mass and then hatch. The young fish, male and female, grow and mature in the surface waters. At a certain point in their development, the male finds a female and bites and holds on to her abdomen. Soon the tissues of the female grow into and attach to the mouth tissues of the male, and the female drops to the bottom of the ocean carrying her parasite male with her not to separate "til death do they part". He found her in the light of the surface waters, so he does not have to grope around in the dark of the deep looking for a mate. How could all of this evolve when it is so ultra-specialized and unique?

Why does the female not chase the male away when he bites her abdomen? Evolution provides no explanation. What possible evolutionary mechanism enables the male's circulatory system to merge with the female's? And from what creature did this peculiar fish evolve? Evolution has no answers.

A major difference between the Angler fish and other fish is the Angler's lack of a swim bladder, which is an air sac to provide buoyancy and to prevent sinking. If it had evolved without an air bladder, it would sink and die. If it had an air bladder and had evolved the bait and light in surface waters, it would be easy prey for other predators and "survival of the fittest" would force it into extinction.

Another feature of the deep sea Angler is its special body, which is designed to prevent crushing. A pressure of over 2,000 pounds per square inch is exerted on the body of the fish at one mile deep. It survives this great pressure with no problem. On the other hand, if the first Anglers were surface fish and lost their air bladders, (through let's say, some unexplainable genetic mutation) and then sank to the bottom of the sea, they would have been crushed. Dead animals don't evolve any further.

The deep-sea Angler had to have been created with all its special equipment fully functional. God says that as we study His creation, it should cause our thoughts to focus on the Creator and to give Him thanks and honor Him as God (Romans 1).[67]

---

[67] For a super treatment of the Angler fish and other highly specialized animals read: *The Natural Limits to Biological Change*, by Lane P. Lester and Raymond G. Bohlin (Zondervan, 1984).

7

EARTH'S PRE-FLOOD
WATER CANOPY

I can remember one particular lunch period sitting in my office at Baylor College of Dentistry studying Genesis 1. Those dental students had asked me to explain to them what God meant in verses 6-8a. How often we read the Bible but don't really think about what it says. As I studied these verses, I realized that I didn't know quite what they were saying. Here is what the Bible says:

"And God said, Let there be a firmament in the midst of the waters, and let it divide the waters from the waters.

And God made the firmament, and divided the waters which were under the firmament from the waters which were above the firmament: and it was so.

And God called the firmament Heaven." (Gen.1:6-8a)

It says God divided the waters and put some water above the firmament (heaven 1:8a) and left some water under the firmament. What is this firmament? Genesis 1:20 reads:

"And God said, Let the waters bring forth abundantly the moving creature that hath life, and fowl that may fly above the earth in the open firmament of heaven."

The expanse or firmament of Genesis 1:7 may be the open heavens of Genesis 1:20 where the birds fly around. Now, there are several views and different interpretations in these Genesis verses, but the one that seems to make the most sense to me is this: God separated the waters that covered the earth in the beginning and left some on earth and put some up above where the birds fly. If this water was in the form of water vapor, it would have made the heaven and earth system #1 similar to a giant terrarium. There would have been no rain! And what does the Bible say? Genesis 2:6: **"But there went up a mist from the earth, and watered the whole face of the ground."** That is the exact effect expected if the earth was surrounded by a water vapor canopy: a morning mist would form. Genesis 2:5b is more specific: **"...for the Lord God had not caused it to rain upon the earth."** No rain, therefore no rainbow! Heaven and earth system #1 was obviously different from our present system, system #2.

The rainbow was the perfect object for God to use as the sign of His covenantal promise of no more global floods. Noah had never seen a rainbow <u>in the clouds</u> before the flood, because it had never rained. After the flood, when the canopy had collapsed during the forty days and nights of rain, Noah was in heaven and earth system #2, and was therefore experiencing our weather: rain and rainbows. He also would experience the difference between pre-flood system #1's heavy atmospheric pressure and system #2's post-flood lighter atmospheric pressure -- the latter causing rapid fermentation of alcohol and quite possibly the reason for Noah's drunkenness.

This pre-flood canopy probably consisted of water vapor. There are other theories, but we must keep in mind that the birds were flying in the expanse under this water, and one must be able to see through the water. The sun, moon and stars were visible to Adam and to Noah, in view of the fact that Genesis 1:14 states that they would serve as signs.

Water vapor is clear, unlike clouds or steam. A little experiment to prove this point can be accomplished in your kitchen by filling a tea-kettle with water and putting it on the stove to boil. When steam begins coming out of the spout, look closely at the very tip of the spout. You will see about one-half to one inch of clear 212°F. water vapor before it becomes cloudy steam. This may have been the form of the water that God put above the firmament in which the birds flew around.

THE GREENHOUSE EFFECT

With a water-vapor canopy, heaven and earth system #! would be considerably different than our present system (#2). A greenhouse effect would be expected due to the heat generated by the sun-warmed canopy. Is there any evidence that greenhouse warmth once surrounded our globe? Palm tree fossils have been found in Alaska and broad leaf ferns in the Arctic. How could a palm tree fossil be in Alaska? Some scientists have postulated they travelled there on the tectonic plate (earth crust) movement over millions of years. But these trees are not millions of years old! A creationist would say, "No problem, palm trees grew in Alaska in the tropical world before the Flood." These trees were buried during the Flood of Noah's day resulting in their fossilization.

Scientists have found tropical forests and coal deposits in Antarctica. Ninety-foot plum trees which were quick frozen and over ninety feet in height with green leaves have been found in the New Siberian islands where, today, only one-inch high willows grow [see Charles Hapgood, The Mystery of the Frozen Mammoths; from Bassett Digby, The Mammoth and Mammoth Hunting Grounds in Northeast Siberia (N.Y.: Appleton, 1926), pp. 150-151].

In these frigid zones many trees, some fossilized and some quick-frozen, have been found with rings, signifying rapid, warm temperature growth. The Evolutionist asks, "How did they get here?" The Creationist says, "They grew there before the Flood when the earth was pole to pole greenhouse warm."

The water vapor canopy may have more than doubled atmospheric pressure on earth. In this environment of heavier atmospheric pressure, healing would be more efficient. Many hospitals have pressurized rooms called Hyperbaric Rooms. Into these rooms oxygen is pumped under pressure and healing is miraculously speeded up. Very sick people and the severely burned are treated in this high pressure environment.[68] In the pre-flood, high efficiency atmosphere, reptiles could have grown to immense sizes, giant flying creatures could have flown more easily, and gigantism would have been much more likely.[69]

---

[68] For more information about "Hyperbaric Therapy" see: J. C. Davis, "Hyperbaric Oxygen Therapy," *Journal of Intensive Care Medicine*, 4 (1989), 55-57. Also: *Textbook of Hyperbaric Medicine*, ed. K. K. Jain (Toronto: Hogrefe and Huber Pubs., 1990), p. 492. Also: *Hyperbaric Oxygen Therapy: A Committee Report (UHMS PUB 30 CRHOB)*, ed. J. T. Mader (Bethesda: Undersea and Hyperbaric Medical Society, Inc., 1989), p. 90.

[69] Most of my comments about the effects of the vapor canopy came from Dr. Joseph Dillow's excellent discussion of the effects of the vapor canopy in *The Water's Above: Earth's Pre-Flood Water Vapor Canopy* (Moody Press, 1982).

THE GREAT DINOSAUR MYSTERY

Evolution has a problem called The Great Dinosaur Mystery. Where did the great dinosaurs come from; how did they grow so big; and, if it is "survival of the fittest", why did these powerful creatures become extinct?

A creationist would answer, "no problem". God created the giant reptiles and may have referred to one or two of them which existed in Job's day (see Job 40:15 - 41:34). Reptiles do not have a built-in growth inhibiting factor like other animals and man. The dinosaurs would have continued growing as long as they lived. The older they got, the bigger they grew. Reptiles function best, as cold-blooded animals, in warm temperature climates. God created large reptiles which kept growing in an efficient high pressure atmosphere with plenty of warmth and unlimited supplies of lush vegetation to eat and nothing to eat them. The Bible says,

> **"And to every beast of the earth, and to every fowl of the air, and to every thing that creepeth upon the earth, wherein there is life, I have given every green herb for meat...."** (Genesis 1:30)

This indicates that all animals ate plants, not flesh, before the Flood. Plants themselves are a testimony to God's creative genius. They start as a seed and take dirt, water, air and sunshine and are converted into roses, rubber and rhubarb! And these incredible factories not only do not pollute the environment, but they silently clean the air and replenish it with life-supporting oxygen. Oh, the wonders of the God of all creation! It was only after the flood that God gave permission to eat flesh **"Every moving thing that liveth shall be meat for you; even as the green herb have I given you all things"** (Genesis 9:3). Nothing ate the dinosaurs before the Flood, and they had bounteous vegetation as food.   They, therefore, could grow to great size during a long lifetime of hundreds of years.   Even Tyrannosaurus rex ate plants, not other dinosaurs, before the flood.   The textbook pictures of this great dinosaur eating another reptile are not based on scientific method and are not supported with factual information.   The three to five inch long teeth of the Tyrannosaurus rex have roots which are too short to support a meat-tearing, bone-crunching diet. Tyrannosaurus most probably was a vegetarian (at least before the flood of Noah, Genesis 1:29, 30) and used his long sharp teeth to strip leaves from plants. After the flood, these reptiles could never grow so huge.   The lighter atmosphere (the weighty canopy came down as rain water at the flood), cooler average temperature and predators would prevent long life and excessive size.

By the way, did you know that there never was a dinosaur called "Brontosaurus"?   Brontosaurus fooled the scientific community for many, many years. It turned out to be the head of one creature and the body of another. The evolutionary community was too embarrassed to admit this mistake for more than fifty years. Brontosaurus does not appear in most new textbooks.

In recent years some evolutionists have postulated that dinosaurs were warm-blooded, not cold-blooded creatures. Warm-blooded dinosaurs have been proposed because scientists are beginning to realize that 300,000 pound cold-blooded creatures do not and could not exist in our environment. There is not enough air pressure to enable their blood to circulate properly. Somehow an important fact has escaped the notice of these evolutionists (or they are "willingly ignorant," II Peter 3:5). The fact is these huge reptiles would have had no problem thriving in the warm, high pressure atmosphere of system #1. The big ones went into extinction after the Great Flood. It is not politically correct for an evolutionist to believe that the universal Flood of Noah's day actually happened. Belief in the Flood is grounds for dismissal from your job or cancellation of your grants. So the evolutionist is left to speculate regarding "The Great Dinosaur Mystery", whereas the creationist has a valid, scientifically testable position -- the environmental differences between system #1 and system #2.

Evolutionists may have theorized that warm-blooded dinosaurs would solve their dilemma, but recent research indicates that the giant reptiles were cold-blooded as are all reptiles to this day. The <u>Dallas Morning News</u> of March 21, 1994 (p.9-D) reported that three University of Pennsylvania paleontologists have published their view (in <u>Nature</u> magazine) that ..."dinosaurs...were probably cold-blooded..."

This is a blow to the evolutionist's dream of solving the mystery of these huge creatures! Of course if you wait a few days some other evolutionary scientist will refute his colleagues' position. Evolutionists keep batting this "warm-blooded" or "cold-blooded" idea back and forth. The <u>Dallas Morning News</u> of July 11, 1994 (page 7-D) published a review by science reporter Matt Crenson of a July 1994 <u>Nature</u> magazine article. The review is partially quoted here:

> "Tyrannosaurus rex had a stable body temperature, a new study shows, suggesting that the largest terrestrial carnivore was warm-blooded.
>
> Reese E. Barrick and William J. Showers of North Carolina State University in Raleigh studied Tyrannosaurus bones uncovered in the rocks of the Hell Creek Formation in eastern Montana...
>
> The remarkable consistency of the oxygen isotopes in the dinosaur's bones demonstrate that its body temperature never varied by more than about 7 degrees Fahrenheit, the North Carolina researchers wrote last week in <u>Nature</u>. If Montana's seasons were anywhere near as variable 70 million years ago, when Tyrannosaurus lived, as they are today, a creature with such a stable body temperature would have had to be warm-blooded."

A creationist might say that a stable body temperature in a giant cold-blooded reptile is consistent with the creationist view that the earth's temperature was uniformly warm in the tropical pre-Flood heaven and earth system number one. Creationists would expect to find "...remarkable consistency of the oxygen isotopes in the dinosaur's bones...". Apparently these evolutionistic researchers would rather pretend that cold-blooded reptiles were actually warm-blooded than to consider the pre-Flood pole-to-pole greenhouse warm condition of earth (6,000 years ago, not 70 million years ago) as presented by the creationist model.

The giant flying reptiles such as the pterosaurs (pterodactyls and pteranodons) would be unable to fly in our present atmosphere. They needed a heavier atmosphere to get enough air to lift them with their 40 to 50-foot wingspans. Heaven and earth system #1 would have provided the heavier atmospheric pressure necessary for the flight of these huge creatures. Evolutionists say we don't know how these giant reptiles could have flown in our atmosphere. To a creationist, this is not a problem. Heaven and earth system #1, before the water canopy came down at the flood of Noah's day, would have provided the air density needed for these huge creatures to fly. In order to protect their jobs the evolutionists dare not even suggest the global flood of Noah's day as part of the solution to their problems, and yet the Flood supplies the explanation for what we "see".

We even read in our older history books about ancient cultures which taught a global flood.

Gigantism was common in the heavy pre-flood atmosphere. Fossil dragonflies with a 32-inch wingspan have been discovered and would be a frightful bug to hit your windshield! The hornless rhinoceros grew to about "...seventeen feet high and nearly thirty feet long!" [70] Giant

---

[70] Petersen, *Unlocking the Mysteries of Creation*, pp. 28,29.

sabre-toothed tigers, mastodons and woolly mammoths roamed the earth side-by-side with the great dinosaurs.

Man lived during the age of the dinosaurs. In cretaceous rock strata of the Paluxy River bottom near Glen Rose, Texas, human and dinosaur footprints have been found crisscrossing each other. Much has been said about these footprints because, if authentic, they prove in solid rock that man and dinosaur lived at the same time. If accepted as genuine, they are a fatal blow in rock to evolution. They are proof that evolution is a false speculation of man! Most textbooks claim that the dinosaurs became extinct about 60 or 70 million years before man stepped onto the scene and into his footprints. Dinosaur and human footprints crisscrossing each other in the same rock strata destroys the evolutionary belief that over a period of millions of years man evolved from his ancient reptilian ancestors!

Two Texas scientists have sectioned (cut into slices of rock) one of these human footprints. Carl Baugh and Don Patton discovered that the rock under the footprints shows pressure structures (called laminations). These pressure structures are exactly what a scientist would expect to find surrounding a human footprint! The human prints (and there are many) are not "carved" into the river-bed and neither are the dinosaur prints.[71]

In the summer of 1993 Drs. Patton and Baugh noticed eleven and one-half inch long human footprints (people have feet that big today) stepping along - left, right, left, right - inside giant three-toed dinosaur prints. Someone was

---

[71] For more information about Glen Rose and the human footprints, contact: Dr. Don R. Patton at the Metroplex Institute of Origin Science, Inc. (MIOS), P.O. Box 550953, Dallas, TX 75355-0953 and Dr. Carl E. Baugh at the Creation Evidences Museum and Archaeological Excavations, P.O. Box 309, Glen Rose, Texas 76043 (817) 897-3200.

walking in the soft mud of fresh dinosaur tracks! One of the tracks shows in rock the human footprint beside the dinosaur track. Apparently the person got "side-tracked" and missed one dinosaur print, but got back "on track" for his next step. These footprints are conclusive, hard, observable evidence that man and dinosaurs walked the earth simultaneously. For a while The Humanist magazine had discredited these Paluxy River footprints to the extent that creationists withdrew their articles and films (a good film documenting the footprints is entitled Footprints in Stone). The summer of 1993 work by Drs. Baugh and Patton should put the shoe back on the other foot! Contact Dr. Don Patton for the incredible account of how several of the footprints (but not all) were destroyed by an overly threatened evolutionist attempting to "...suppress the truth...".

Proverbs 14:12 tells us that **"There is a way which seemeth right unto a man, but the end thereof are the ways of death."** Evolutionists travel to Glen Rose, Texas and examine the human and dinosaur footprints side by side or overlapped with each other in cretaceous rock, and they concoct foolish speculations rather than bow their knees and heads before their Creator who told us all that dinosaurs and humans existed together on the sixth day of the creation week. The Bible teaches that man and dinosaur shared the same earth at the same time (Genesis 1). This presents no difficulty since those giant creatures ate only plants before the Flood! In the early days of His creation, God prevented animals from eating each other or man, since He purposed to fill the earth with His creatures.

Another evidence to support the fact that people and dinosaurs lived at the same time in history is the cave paintings of dinosaurs. How could a "pre-historic" man or woman paint a picture of a dinosaur if he or she had never seen one? The Institute for Creation Research (ICR) circulates an excellent video documenting the cave drawings of dinosaurs.

LONGEVITY OF LIFE

Another result of the water (vapor?) being above the firmament in which the birds fly would be the shielding effect from cosmic radiation. Scientists have studied how much solar radiation is filtered by water. Their conclusions are reported by Dr. Joseph Dillow in his book, The Waters Above: Earth's Pre-Flood Water Vapor Canopy. In heaven and earth system #1, people could live to be very old. One of the primary aging factors is solar radiation. By filtering out the harmful radiation (as a water canopy would do) humans might be able to live close to 1,000 years.

The Bible reports that Adam died at 930 years of age and Methuselah lived almost 1,000 years. After the flood, the ages of people dropped off drastically to an average of 70 to 80 years. A lot of people think that you cannot believe the Bible when it says people lived to be 800 or 900 years old -- that it must be a different kind of year or the writer did not know quite what he was talking about. Those old ages are 360-day years just like the Bible says (compare Genesis 7:11 and 8:3,4).[72] You can believe the Bible as it is written. Some present-day researchers who study longevity of life believe that humans could live that long again if we were sheltered from the harmful effects of the sun and the now polluted air.

---

[72] In Genesis 7:11, the flood began on the seventeenth day of the second month and in the seventh month on the seventeenth day (five months later) as recorded in Genesis 8:4, the ark rested on Ararat. According to Genesis 8:3, these five months included 150 days -- 150 days divided by five months = 30 days in a month; 30 days x 12 months = 360 days in an Old Testament year.

Solar shielding by the water canopy above the atmosphere where the birds fly would also affect dating techniques. Negligible amounts of carbon 14 would have formed before the flood.[73] That means that carbon 14 dating techniques would be totally worthless after 5,000 years or so. More about dating techniques later.

---

[73] The Institute for Creation Research is most helpful and has several different publications dealing with dating techniques. Every family should subscribe to the I.C.R. monthly newsletter, *Acts and Facts*, Institute for Creation Research, P.O. Box 2667, El Cajon, CA 92021 (619) 448-0900.

MARVEL OF GOD'S CREATION #7
The Beaver

The beaver is another uniquely designed creation. The following is copied verbatim from <u>Creation Ex Nihilo</u> Vol. 15 No. 2, March-May 1993, pages 38-41. Hopefully you will see the value of subscribing to this creationist magazine as you read the words of author and scientist, Denis Dreves:

"Beavers: Aquatic Architects"

"The dam building ability of beavers is fairly well known, but beavers possess other amazing design features which God has included in their anatomy. Beavers are air-breathing mammals which spend a great deal of time in water. For this reason they need special equipment.

First, the beaver has special valves in its ears and nose. When the beaver dives below the water these valves automatically close so that no water can enter. When the animal resurfaces, the valves reopen and it breathes again.

Perhaps their most amazing piece of equipment is their eyelids. If you have done any diving or snorkeling you will know that water and materials in it can irritate your eyes and wash out natural lubricants. Not only that, but your eyes do not see well under water. That is why snorkelers wear goggles.

Were we original to think up this idea of goggles?

Not really. God designed beavers with "built-in" goggles. Their eyelids are transparent, so they can close their eyes underwater and still see extremely well. Their transparent eyelids give protection to their eyes from waterborne irritants.

During winter, beavers must feed on the bark of trees they have cut and stored in the autumn, using their specially designed, self-sharpening front incisors (perhaps one of the beaver's better known pieces of equipment).

The beavers collect the young trees [usually two to five centimeters (one to two inches) in diameter] for food, cut them to suitable lengths and then transport them, by holding them in their teeth, to their underwater cache, forcing the branches into the mud at the bottom of the pond.

AMAZING DESIGN

Which brings us to another amazing design feature. To retrieve the stored food in the winter months when ice covers the pond, the beaver may need to chew the sticks underwater. They can do this without water entering their mouths, because they have fur mouth flaps between their front incisors and their rear molar teeth, which are set considerably further back. These two folds of skin, one on each side of the mouth, meet behind the incisors and seal off the rest of the mouth.

The beaver's large paddle-shaped tail, which has a scale-like skin covering it, is used as a rudder when it swims. This is particularly important when the animal is swimming with a branch in its mouth. The tail must compensate for any uneven drag from the branch, thus the tail is often held at an angle for accurate steering.

The rear feet of the beaver are large and webbed like a duck's feet, to give the animal good swimming ability. The two inner claws of each foot have split toenails, which the beaver uses as a comb to groom itself and oil its fur.

Beavers use their smaller, unwebbed front paws to carry mud and other materials, and to dig canals which they use as a means of transporting wood and also as a means of quick escape from predators.

The fur of the beaver must be oiled to prevent water reaching the animal's skin. The oil is provided from two large oil glands. They are filled with a rich, thick, deep yellow oily liquid, which the beaver spreads on its fur for waterproofing. This, along with its two layers of fur, are so effective that water rarely reaches the skin. A layer of fat beneath the skin gives further protection against the cold.

A beaver can swim submerged for perhaps 800 meters (a half-mile) or more. Most air-breathing creatures would be adversely affected by lack of oxygen to the brain. The beaver has special equipment to compensate for this need. Large lungs and liver allow for the storage of more air and oxygenated blood. In addition, a beaver's heart beats more slowly when it dives, in order to conserve oxygen, and the blood is restricted to the animals extremities while the vital supply to the brain remains normal.

ENGINEERING SKILLS

Beavers construct dams that may be hundreds of meters long. Construction of the dam is done by cutting down trees and shrubs, dragging each piece to the dam-site, and laying them in the water parallel to the stream (end facing upstream). Almost everything the beavers can find goes into the dam - live wood, dead wood, mud, grass and rocks. When the beaver's pond floods, mounting pressure on the dam can cause it to break. To prevent this, if there is time, the beaver engineers a spillway to relieve pressure, then fixes it after the water subsides.

Beaver lodges are also the work of a master builder. They are built with sticks, and sealed from the cold with mud. The center of the roof is not sealed, which allows some ventilation. Access is only from underwater, with more than one entry in case of the need to escape. The beavers can gain direct underwater access to the cache of sticks they have stored under the water when ice covers the pond in winter and this is their only available food.

Truly the beaver is yet another example of the wonderful provision and wise planning of a caring Creator God. Such variety of essential equipment could not have evolved over time by chance and selection. All of the beaver's equipment must be present and fully functional in the animal from the beginning for it to survive its semi-aquatic life-style."

8

THE COLLAPSE
OF THE WATER CANOPY

What might have caused the water vapor canopy to come down as rain? Several theories exist, although, of course, God does not need a naturalistic cause; He could just sovereignly command the rains of the flood to pour down by His omnipotent power.

One proposed idea for the precipitation of the rain is that a meteorite slammed into the earth, shooting great clouds of dust up into the water vapor. The dust particles would provide the nuclei of condensation for the raindrops and down comes the canopy. Along with this idea is the suggestion that the earth tipped 23 1/2 degrees off dead center during this meteor's impact, resulting in frozen ice-caps and the four seasons.

Another theory holds that a large number of volcanoes erupted simultaneously around the earth, and the volcanic dust provided the particles for the condensation of the vapor into rain. Perhaps all of these cataclysmic events were happening at the same time -- the meteor hit the earth, fracturing the earth's crust, which in turn gave birth to multiple volcanoes.

If there were volcanic activity at the time of the flood, then volcanic ash would be expected in deep, old ice and frozen muck. In the antarctic[74] and arctic, the oldest ice and muck is saturated with volcanic ash. The creationist position holds water.

A sudden and permanent temperature drop from pole-to-pole greenhouse warm (heaven and earth system #1) to frozen ice-caps and moderate temperature (heaven and earth system #2) would occur during the canopy collapse and Flood. In 1893, just one volcano, Krakatau,[75] lowered the average global temperature five degrees for a year. Dust from Krakatau shot 30 miles up into the atmosphere and a series of tidal waves washed across the seas with the greatest being 120 feet high. This incredible wave pushed several miles inland on Java and Sumatra.

If the dust from one volcano could lower the temperature of the earth for an entire year, what might be the chaos and cataclysm of hundreds of volcanoes erupting simultaneously? Could it be that the Bible is describing volcanic activity when it tells us that on the seventeenth day of the second month: **"...the same day were all the fountains of the great deep broken up,..." (Genesis 7:11)**? This was the first day of a sudden and permanent

---

[74] See Anthony Gow, "Glaciological Investigations in Antarctica," *Antarctic Journal of U.S.*, Vol. 7 No. 4 (1972),100-101.

[75] Cheryl Simon, "Krakatau 1893: The Shock Felt 'Round the World'," *Science News*, 124 (May, 1983), 138.

temperature drop, the effects of which are in evidence to this day.

Science News (July 6, 1991, Vol. 140, #1, p. 7) headlines:

"VOLCANO COULD COOL CLIMATE, REDUCE OZONE."

The article states: "The eruption of Mt. Pinatubo could chill the Earth slightly for the next few years and hasten the destruction of the ozone layer over large portions of the world, say scientists...." (p. 7). Scientific literature refers to the "Ring of Fire". Several thousand years ago, volcanoes erupted simultaneously all around the world. What caused this cataclysmic ring of fire? Could this have been the "seventeenth day of the second month"?

QUICK FROZEN ANIMALS

Evolutionary science has no answer for the existence of many quick-frozen animals found in various places around the globe. Among these frozen animals are rhinoceros, hyena, oxen, sabre-toothed tigers, hippopotamus, bison, donkeys, leopards, ibex and giant woolly mammoths. What is a quick-frozen rhinoceros doing in Siberia? Is it that he was on a little summer vacation and before he could get back to Africa, got caught in a freezing blizzard? No, there were tropical animals living in Siberia before the Flood of Noah's day! The earth was pole-to-pole greenhouse warm under the water canopy. This presents an immense problem for evolutionists. What happened back then to quick-freeze tropical plants and animals in Siberia? None of these frozen "fossil" animals are transitional-form animals. All of these very ancient animals are discrete entities. They are instantly and easily classified as bison or mammoths. "Well", say evolutionists, "It must have been a slowly creeping ice age that caught up to these animals."

The frozen animal remains do not represent a slowly creeping ice age. They were caught and <u>permanently</u> frozen (they are still frozen today) with such incredible speed that undigested plants remained in their mouths and in their stomach's digestive juices. Giant nine-ton mammoths have been discovered with undigested buttercups in their mouths and in their stomachs which are still identifiable as to genus and species of the plant! (see Dillow, footnote #68)

What would it take to quick-freeze a happy, healthy nine-ton mammoth grazing on buttercups (and several hundred other identifiable plants which no longer grow in the frigid climate where the frozen mammoths are found)? Some scientists went to a major food-freezing company and posed this question. The answer does not fit into the known realities of heaven and earth system #2 (our present system).

To quick-freeze nine tons of warm blooded animal munching on buttercups, it would take a temperature of -175°F (the coldest temperature ever recorded on earth is near -128°F), a wind-chill factor of a 200-400 m.p.h. wind, over a time of about four hours (eight hours at the outside limit). The problem is that there is nothing on earth that approaches these conditions necessary to freeze the animals -- and yet the animals are frozen. To preserve the meat and undigested plants, drastic conditions not known on our present earth would have been necessary for the quick-freeze. The freezing of these ancient plants and animals was not caused by a slowly creeping ice age. Many textbooks will show an artist's imaginary picture of a mammoth standing in a blizzard with a slowly creeping glacier moving up from behind. This is imagination, not reality. The mammoths were warm-temperature animals, eating warm-temperature plants in a warm-temperature climate that suddenly, in a matter of hours, became permanently frozen.

Another interesting fact about mammoths is documented by M. L. Ryder:

> "The scarcity of hair in the modern elephant is associated with a corrugation of the epidermis, and a lack of skin glands. Although the mammoth, too,...lacked glands, the increase of the hair was associated with a loss of the epidermal corrugation....
> Sections cut parallel to the skin surface revealed sparse, round, non-medullated hairs with no glands or erector muscles." [76]

Mammoth skin has been dissected and, to the surprise of evolutionists, it contains no sebaceous (oil) glands. Why should this be a surprise? Because cold temperature animals have a plentiful supply of oil glands to oil their hair and fur. Wolves, polar bears and seals have such oily fur that the frigid northern water rolls off and does not penetrate to the skin. Cold temperature animals need a lot of oil to protect them from the wet cold. A mammoth could not last very long in a frigid climate without oil in its hair. It was a warm-temperature animal eating warm-temperature plants that was caught suddenly and frozen quickly and permanently in the distant past. Evolution provides no answer for this! A slowly creeping ice age is not a sufficient explanation for the quick-frozen animals -- but a cataclysm such as would have resulted with the collapse of the canopy at the Flood of Noah's day provides the answer and the evidence.

An animal with no oil glands in its skin cannot survive in a frigid climate. But an animal with oil glands can survive in frigid or tropical climates. Leopards have oil glands and can survive in tropical climates. Yet, their pelts have been used to make fur coats that are quite warm in winter. Polar bears survive in zoos in the intense summer heat of southern states.

---

[76] M. L. Ryder, "Hair of the Mammoth," *Nature*, 249 (May 10, 1974), 190,191.

These mammoths (and many other animals) were frozen so quickly that their meat can still be eaten.

> "In many instances, as is well known, entire carcasses of the mammoth have been found thus buried, with the hair, skin and flesh as fresh as in frozen New Zealand sheep in the hold of a steamer. And sleigh dogs as well as Yakuts themselves, have often made a hearty meal of mammoth flesh thousands of years old." [77]

This sudden and permanent temperature change from pole-to- pole greenhouse warm to the present perma-frost or permanent ice condition at and near the poles could have happened during the collapse of the water canopy at the Flood-judgment of God in the days of Noah. The frozen condition, since the break-up of the canopy permitted heat to escape our atmosphere, has preserved for us animal and plant life (now extinct) which existed in heaven and earth system #1. Evolution has no good answer for the sudden death of the frozen animals. The Bible would lead us to believe these things happened at the Flood destruction of system #1.

The Bible gives us a warning in Colossians 2:8:

"Beware lest any man spoil you through philosophy and vain deceit, after the tradition of men, after the rudiments of the world, and not after Christ."

Evolution is a philosophical system and an empty deception.[78]   Christians should not be taken captive by

---

[77] G. Richard Lydekker, "Mammoth Ivory," *Smithsonian Reports* (1899), p. 363, as reported by Dr. Joseph Dillow, *The Waters Above*, p. 312. (See footnote #69)

[78] When we depart from the simplicity and purity of devotion to Christ (II Cor. 11:3), we accept empty deceptions. Many Christians have departed from Biblical Truth to believe in Darwinian evolution or in Punctuated Equilibrium (evolution did not happen too slow to see, it happened too fast to see). Stephen Jay Gould and Niles Eldredge promote "Punctuated Equilibria" as the mode of evolution (see: "Punctuated Equilibria: the Tempo and Mode of Evolution

evolution -- there is no <u>factual</u> science (science not based on assumptions, see Dr. Kerkut's assumptions in Chapter 2, page 21) to support the molecules-to-man model of origins. In studying origins (where we came from) we must keep in mind that both evolution and creation are faith systems. We have allowed ourselves to be brainwashed into believing that scientific facts prove evolution of molecules-to-man to be true. No one but God was there when the universe and life appeared. Let us not be led astray from the simplicity and purity of devotion to Christ! (II Cor. 11:3)

1.   Praise Ye the Lord. Praise ye the Lord from the heavens: praise him in the heights!

2.   Praise ye him, all his angels: praise ye him, all his hosts.

3.   Praise ye him, sun and moon: praise him, all ye stars of light.

4.   Praise him, ye heavens of heavens, and ye waters that *be* above the heavens.

5.   Let them praise the name of the Lord: for he commanded, and they were created. (Psalm 148:1-5)

Reconsidered," *Paleobiology*, 3 (Spring 1977). The punctuated equilibria model (evolution is too fast to see) has been around for a long time even though Gould seems to accept praise as the "father" of it. Punctuated equilibria is foundational to Marxist-Leninism and was seen by Marx and Lenin as essential to move people away from Biblical Truth into the vain philosophy and empty deception of Marxist-Leninism. For excellent documentation of this and Gould's roots as a Marxist, read:
The Long War Against God by Dr. Henry Morris (Baker Book House, 1989), and *Understanding the Times* by Dr. David Noebel (Summit Ministries, Box 207, Manitou Springs, Colorado 80829, 1991).

MARVEL OF GOD'S CREATION #8
The Chicken Egg

A fertilized chicken egg is a very special creation. Before even thinking about a chick developing in an egg, it is interesting to ponder how the chicken manages to get a shell around that slippery, raw, fertilized egg. It is a rare sight on the farm to see raw egg smeared on the outside of the shell. Have you ever attempted to put an egg back into its shell after it rolled off the counter?

The shell itself is highly specialized. Each egg shell has about 10,000 tiny holes or pores. How does that chicken form a shell around a soft, messy egg and design the shell to have porosity? Put a raw egg in warm water and soon you will see tiny bubbles floating up. These bubbles are escaping through the pores in the shell. The developing chick needs these pores to breathe. Evolution requires a need before an organism will change. How does a chicken know it needs to make a shell with porosity, and how can it manufacture such a shell? The chick does not know it needs the holes in the shell to breathe until it dies for lack of air. Of course, dead chicks cannot evolve.

Within the first few days after the egg is laid, blood vessels begin to grow out of the developing chick. Two of these attach to the membrane under the eggshell and two attach to the yolk. By the fifth day, the tiny heart is pumping blood through the vessels. What makes those blood vessels grow out of the chick, and how do they know where to go and to what to attach?

The chick feeds from the yolk with the yolk vessels and breathes through the membrane vessels. If any of these vessels do not grow out of the chick or attach to the correct place, the chick will die.

The chick gives off carbon dioxide and water vapor as it metabolizes the yolk. If it does not get rid of the carbon dioxide and water vapor, it will die of gaseous poisoning or drown in its own waste water. These waste products are picked up by the blood vessels and leave through the pores in the eggshell.

By the nineteenth day, the chick is too big to get enough oxygen through the pores in the shell. It must do something or die. How does it know what to do next? By this time, a small tooth called the "egg-tooth" has grown onto its beak. It uses this little tooth to peck a hole into the air sack at the flat end of the egg. When you peel a hard-boiled egg you notice the thin membrane under the shell and the flattened end of the egg. This flattened end, which looks like the hen did not quite fill up her egg shell, is the air sack. The air sack provides only six hours of air for the chick to breathe. Instead of relaxing and breathing deeply, with this new-found supply of air, the chick keeps pecking until it breaks a small hole through the shell to gain access to outside air in adequate amounts.

On the twenty-first day, the chick breaks out of the shell. If one step in the development of the chick is missing or out of order, the chick dies.[79]

Each step in the development of the chick defies evolutionary logic. The process must be orchestrated by God, our Creator. The impersonal plus time plus chance is

---

[79] Bob Devine, *God In Creation* (Chicago: Moody Press, 1982), pp. 9-13. This booklet discusses ten of God's creations and shows how they could not have evolved. There are a series of these booklets.

not an adequate explanation for the incredible complexities of life as we observe it.

9

DO MUTATIONS PRODUCE NEW LIFE FORMS?

When I began to feel the pressure of having no experimentally testable facts to substantiate my position as a theistic evolutionist, I turned to what I thought was my ace in the hole: Genetics. Didn't everyone know that the science of genetics had irrevocably shown evolution in progress? Without mutations (changes in the genes and chromosomes), there is no evolutionary change. The question my students asked was, "Do mutations produce new life forms or improvements in present life forms?" Naturally I assumed they produce new forms and I thought I could prove it from the scientific literature. I was due for another rude awakening!

Many creationists[80] and evolutionists study the phenomenon of genetic mutation. The predominant view of evolutionists was expressed by Dr. Ernst Mayr of Harvard: "Ultimately, all variation is, of course, due to mutation." [81] Dr. Mayr instructs us that all variation (different types of plants and animals) observable in life is due to changes in the genes and chromosomes. These mutations occur in the make-up of DNA.

DNA: LANGUAGE OF THE CELL

DNA, the basic information system of the cell, contains the blue prints needed to manufacture twenty or more different proteins. Each of these proteins is manufactured in little "cell-factories" at the direction of the DNA and is essential for the maintenance of life. So, which came first? If DNA is essential in the manufacturing process of proteins, and the manufacturing process produces the proteins essential to DNA, then you can't have one without the other. This means they both must have been created fully functional and at exactly the same point in time. In other words, God must have created the information system of all cells at a point in time <u>and</u> fully functional. DNA is needed to make DNA! DNA provides the instructions to the chemical factories inside the cell for making itself.

Scientists call DNA the "language of the cell." All scientists agree that language requires intelligence. Could there be an implication here that DNA, the "language of the

---

[80] Dr. Walter Brown wrote a paper several years ago on the evidences for creation. In his footnotes was a selection of quotes from the pro-evolutionary literature dealing with genetics. For this valuable information, please contact Dr. Walter Brown, The Center for Scientific Creation, 5612 North 20th Place, Phoenix, AZ 85016.

[81] Ernst Mayr, *Mathematical Challenges to the Neo-Darwinian Interpretation of Evolution* (Philadelphia: Wister Institute Press, 1967), p. 50.

cell" required intelligence to create it? Could it be that DNA was created fully functional in all the different kinds of life by an intelligent Designer, the God of the Bible! Evolution offers no answers to this weighty problem. Yet the God of Creation proclaims through His Holy Scriptures, "I created, created, created!"

The genetic information of DNA cannot be improved upon in any normal, healthy organism. Natural selection or "survival of the fittest" does not produce new genes, it merely selects the best suited animal or plant life for a specific niche or environment. This is adaptation to a specific environment and not mutation. Yet mutation is the only mechanism scientists have proposed to generate the "new" genetic information needed for evolutionary change in the molecules-to-man model. This presents an enormous problem for the evolution model, especially when we learn that mutation in a gene is a rare event.[82]

How could life have evolved into all its millions of forms if the very mechanism that causes it to evolve (mutation) is a rare event? When mutations do occur, geneticists tell us that mutations are 99.9% harmful.

> "The process of mutation is the only source of the raw materials of genetic variability, and hence, of evolution....The mutants which arise are, with rare exceptions, deleterious to their carriers, at least in the environments which the species normally encounters." (Theodosius Dobzhansky) [83]

Dobzhansky spent his professional life breeding and mutating fruit flies. In the end, he had somewhat strange

---

[82] "Although mutation is the ultimate source of all genetic variation, it is a relatively rare event..." , Francisco Ayala, "The Mechanics of Evolution," *Scientific American*, September 1978, p. 63.

[83] Theodosius Dobzhansky, "On Methods of Evolutionary Biology and Anthropology," *American Scientist*, Winter, December 1957, p. 385.

fruit flies, but fruit flies nonetheless. Some of those flies were not even able to reproduce because they had become sterile. Dobzhansky writes that mutations are the only source of evolution, but that they are almost always harmful (which means the mutation makes the life-form that gets it less able to survive where it lives). If "survival of the fittest" is true, then mutations should cause extinctions not new and better life forms. Of course what we observe in nature are extinctions of plants and animals rather than emerging, new life forms. There are millions of living things from plants to insects, but we hear almost weekly of more extinctions. How many newly evolved creatures have you heard about in your lifetime? With all the millions of living things in the world surely mutations are happening and something is or has evolved into something else. The evolutionists are frantically searching for the smallest hint that something will evolve and prove their theory to be true.

A few years ago the evolutionary community presented to the public their best example of evolution in progress. It was a guppy family that had been separated from their old friends for several years. When the guppies were reunited they would not mate. Evolutionists consider a life-form to be a new species when it will no longer mate with its old friends. Maybe the guppy didn't smell good when it came back from its temporary environment. Or maybe its old friends didn't recognize it, or maybe the researchers didn't wait long enough to see if the guppy would be accepted again. The fact is that both populations of guppies were still unmistakably identifiable to scientists and laymen as guppies. Where is the evidence for the evolution of one creature into another when after more than eleven years of breeding guppies they are still guppies.

Even if these fish refuse to breed with each other and are therefore categorized as a new species of guppy, does this prove evolution of one kind into another kind of creature.

People have devised their definitions of and limits to species, but God refers to "kinds" in the Genesis account. Biblically, there are certain boundaries that no living form can cross. A specific "kind" of creature will never evolve into another "kind" of creature. Guppies are fish. Within the fish-kind there is a lot of room for change, even "evolutionary" change, but fish will forever be fish, big ones, little ones, fresh water and salt water, but still fish.

It doesn't seem right for scientists to tell us in school and college that the chief mechanism in our ever upward and onward evolutionary process is mutation in the genes when they say in the scientific literature mutations are harmful or deadly: "Mutations are more than just sudden changes in heredity; they also affect viability, and, to the best of our knowledge, invariably affect it adversely." (C.P. Martin) [84],[85],[86]

So we learn that mutations in a healthy life-form invariably cause harmful changes or death (lethal) to the organism. How does evolution from molecules-to-man occur if the very process that supposedly causes it to happen, in truth, harms or kills the organism? To put this another way, why did the evolutionary scientists evacuate the area when the Three Mile Island nuclear reactor in Pennsylvania destroyed itself? Why didn't these scientists move their families into the area to be irradiated so mutations might develop and they could evolve into the next higher life form? The scientists knew that their offspring would inherit

---

[84] C. P. Martin, "A Non-Geneticist Looks at Evolution," *American Scientist*, January 1953, p. 162.

[85] "If we say that it is only by chance that they (mutations) are useful, we are still speaking too leniently. In general, they are useless, detrimental, or lethal." W. R. Thompson, *Introduction to the Origin of Species*, by Charles Darwin (New York: E. P. Dutton, 1956), p. 10.

[86] "Lethal mutations outnumber visibles (Albinism, Dwarfism, Hemophilism) by about 20 to 1. Mutations that have harmful effects are even more frequent than lethal ones." A. M. Winchester, *Genetics*, 5th ed. (Boston: Houghton Mufflin Co., 1977), p. 356.

unhealthy characteristics from the Three Mile Island irradiation. They got away from the mutation-causing radiation as fast as they could!

Professor of Genetics at the University of Wisconsin, James Crow writes:

> "...mutants would usually be detrimental. For a mutation is a random change of a highly organized reasonably smoothly functioning living body. A random change in the highly integrated system of chemical processes which constitute life is almost certain to impair it -- just as a random interchange of connections in a television set is not likely to improve the picture." [87]

Dr. Crow's analogy is accurate. All of us know that stirring up and haphazardly reattaching wires in the back of a T.V. set will not improve the picture. In the same way random changes in the genes do not improve our ability to live and function. As a matter of fact no scientist has yet observed a random mutation produce a new hormone, enzyme, or simple organ.[88] Nevertheless they teach us and our children the lie that we are here because our primeval ancestors had mutations occur in their genes that caused them to evolve higher and higher until here we are. Magic!! Listen to the words of the famous evolutionist from the University of Pennsylvania, Dr. Loren Eiseley:

---

[87] James Crow, "Genetic Effects of Radiation," *Bulletin of Atomic Sciences*, 14 (1958), 19-20.

[88] "Do we, therefore, ever see mutations going about the business of producing new structures for selection to work on? No nascent organ has ever been observed emerging, though their origin in prefunctional form is basic to evolutionary theory. Some should be visible today, occurring in organisms at various stages up to integration of a functional new system, but we don't see them: there is no sign at all of this kind of radical novelty. Neither observation or controlled experiment has shown natural selection manipulating mutations so as to produce a new gene, hormone, enzyme system or organ." Michael Pitman, *Adam and Evolution* (London: Rider Press, 1981), pp. 67,68.

"With the failure of these many efforts (to prove evolution to be true), science was left in the somewhat embarrassing position of having to <u>postulate theories of living origins which it could not demonstrate. After having chided the theologian for his reliance on myth and miracle, science found itself in the unenviable position of having to create a mythology of its own</u>: namely, the assumption that what, after long effort could not be proved to take place today had in truth, taken place in the primeval past." [89] (Emphasis added)

PLANT EVOLUTION

One of the world's leading experts on plant evolution and fossil plants, Dr. E. J. H. Corner of Cambridge University dogmatically states:

"The theory of evolution is not merely the theory of the origin of species, but the only explanation of the fact that organisms can be classified into this hierarchy of natural affinity. Much evidence can be adduced in favour of the theory of evolution -- from biology, bio-geography and paleontology, but I still think that, <u>to the unprejudiced, the fossil record of plants is in favour of special creation.</u>" [90] (Emphasis added)

According to expert Corner, there is no evidence for the evolution of plants. In fact, when plants are studied closely they appear to be a special creation! The field of botany (plants) does not prove evolution, and yet Dr. Corner still believes in an evolutionary mythological system. He is trusting his compatriots in "biology, bio-geography and paleontology" to prove evolution to be true. In Corner's field (plants), special creation appears to be the best option.

---

[89] Dr. Loren Eiseley, *The Immense Journey* (New York: Random House, 1957), p. 199.

[90] E. J. H. Corner, *'Evolution' in Contemporary Botanical Thought*, eds. Anna M. Macleod and L. S. Cobley, Oliver and Boyd, for the Botanical Society of Edinburg, 1961, p. 97. As quoted (partially) from *The Quote Book*, p. 11.

If there is no evidence for the evolution of people or plants, then how about evidence for the evolution of fish?

EVOLUTION OF FISH

"The geological record has so far provided no evidence as to the origin of the fishes,...[J.R. Norman (British Museum of Natural History)] [91]

According to these experts, there is no evidence for the evolution of plants, and no evidence for the evolution of fish. What about amphibians?

EVOLUTION OF AMPHIBIANS

"...none of the known fishes is thought to be directly ancestral to the earliest land vertebrates. Most of them lived after the first amphibians appeared, and those that came before show no evidence of developing the stout limbs and ribs that characterized the primitive tetrapods...

Since the fossil material provides no evidence of other aspects of the transformation from fish to tetrapod, paleontologists have had to speculate how legs and aerial breathing evolved..." (Barbara J. Stahl) [92] (Emphasis added).

No evidence for the evolution of plants and no evidence for fish. What's more, the only evidence for amphibians is the "speculations" of the fossil experts. The evidence, then, for evolution of creatures as they supposedly developed the ability to crawl out of water and live as land animals is in the imagination of the evolutionist. There are no fossils and no

---

[91] J. R. Norman, "Classification and Pedigrees: Fossils," in *A History of Fishes*, 3rd ed., ed. Dr. P. H. Greenwood, British Museum of Natural History, London, 1975, p. 343. As quoted (partially) from *The Quote Book*, p. 11.

[92] Barbara J. Stahl, *Vertebrate History: Problems in Evolution* (New York: McGraw-Hill, 1974), pp. 148,195. As quoted in *The Quote Book*, p. 11.

facts to support belief in the evolution of amphibians. How about birds?

EVOLUTION OF BIRDS

"The [evolutionary] origin of birds is largely a matter of deduction. There is no fossil evidence of the stages through which the remarkable change from reptile to bird was achieved." (W.E. Swinton) [93]

The evolution of birds is a "matter of deduction". "Deduction" in this case is a polite synonym for imagination. There is not a single, undisputed fossil that shows the evolutionary transitions of reptiles into birds.

According to the above evolutionary experts, evolution is grossly lacking in hard evidence! Although we are told that mutations are good because they generate new life and produce evolution, we do not see this "good" happening in reality. Genetic mutations cannot be the driving force behind evolution. Nor do the evolutionists provide evidence to prove the evolution of any creature.

TIME GENERATES MIRACLES

But what if earth history was counted in billions of years? The old argument always comes along at this point that anything can happen in a random-chance system if it is given enough time. The miracle of life can come from dead chemicals if given enough time. We will discuss the "billions of years" argument in Chapter 10. But before leaving Chapter 9, let us not forget that changes in the genes

---

[93] Wo. E. Swinton, "The Origin of Birds," Chapter 1 in *Biology and Comparative Physiology of Birds*, A. J. Marshall, ed., Vol. I (New York: Academic Press, 1960), p. 1. As quoted in *The Quote Book*, p. 11.

(random mutations) do not improve present life forms, nor is there any solid factual evidence that they generate new plants or animals.   The evacuation of Three Mile Island spoke volumes! (If, indeed, mutations are helpful then we should gladly and willingly expose ourselves to them to "improve" our evolutionary opportunities!)

MARVEL OF GOD'S CREATION #9
The Chuckwalla Lizard

"Chuckwalla lizards are large, pot-bellied lizards which wear a loose, baggy skin. Though the skin appears to be much too large, it is just exactly what this lizard needs when an enemy approaches. You see, when an enemy comes near the chuckwalla, the lizard runs very quickly to a rock crevice and hides in it. In the crack of the rock, the chuckwalla swallows air and blows up like a balloon. When the enemy arrives the chuckwalla is safely wedged in the crack. Though it is within easy reach, it is safe. Years ago, the Indians of our desert Southwest learned how to catch the chuckwalla. They pierced its body with an arrow to let out the air; then the Indians could easily remove the lizard from its haven. Man is probably the only enemy of the chuckwalla lizard from whom it is not completely safe.

Of course, the desert is very dry. Some chuckwallas live where there may be only a single rain shower in a whole year. In these arid places the chuckwalla generally lives a dormant life for most of the year. It estivates, or sleeps, for all but about five months of the year.

While living actively, the chuckwalla eats whatever juicy plants it can find. Special glands store the water from the greenery, and the chuckwalla grows fat from its food. Generally, chuckwallas are dormant from August through March.

Many desert plants absorb much salt from the soil in which they grow. The chuckwalla receives enough salt from its food to kill an ordinary animal. The salt would kill the chuckwalla, too, were it not for its special salt-removing glands.   These glands are located in the nostrils of the chuckwalla, and, as the salt builds up on the glands, the lizard occasionally sneezes.   The sneeze expels the crystallized salt which the glands have filtered out of the lizard's bloodstream.

The cold-blooded chuckwalla sleeps late. But when it arises, it must warm up in a hurry. Desert nights and early mornings are often very cold. Cold-blooded creatures are slow and sluggish when they are cold, and cold lizards are easy to catch. For this reason, the chuckwalla wears a dark-colored, heat-absorbing skin.   The sun warms the lizard before the air warms up. Later in the day, the lizard's skin changes to a heat-reflecting light color because the chuckwalla must not get too hot either. The rationality we find when we examine the chuckwalla's body structure compels us to recognize its Designer. Only God, Who is an intelligent, rational Being, can account for the order and design evident in the chuckwalla lizard and all of nature." [94]

---

[94] DeWitt Steele, *Science: Order and Reality* (Pensacola, Fl: A Beka Book Publications, 1980), p. 138. Christian parents, do you realize that there are science books that your children can be studying that defend the creationist's perspective?

10

EARTH: YOUNG OR OLD - GIVE ME FACTS, NOT ASSUMPTIONS

When faced with lack of evidence to support their faith system, the evolution of molecules to man, the evolutionist will always fall back on the argument of "time". "Give us enough time," they say, "and evolution will occur." And so the evolutionists publish dates of billions of years for the age of the universe. These "billions and billions of years" are emphasized from our childhood days. As little children, we hear famous people and "credentialed" science writers in white lab coats over and over again and again refer to these long ages of time. News broadcasters and public television nature programs refer to billions of years as a matter of fact.

<u>Repetition is essential to brainwashing; and brainwashing is essential to belief in one-cell-to-man evolution, since there is no factual science (science not based on assumptions) to back it up.</u> Most creationists would say that the universe is somewhere between six and ten thousand years old.   A young universe is not a problem for creationists because our God, the Creator-God of the Bible, is also the Creator of time.   He does not need time.   He can and did create fully mature people, plants and animals.

The evolutionists make major assumptions during the course of determining a date of several million or billion years for the age of a piece of rock.   If any of their assumptions are invalid, then it is impossible to use that technique to find a correct age for the rock.   Here is how these dating techniques work: Let us say we find a rock and then want to determine how old it is.   We decide to analyze the rock by looking for certain elements or compounds which break down over time into certain other elements or compounds.   We might look for a special isotope of uranium and the element it eventually breaks down (decays) into, which is a special isotope of lead.   In our rock specimen, we find some of this special uranium and some of the lead it decays into (the "daughter" element).   The lead is called the daughter element because it comes from the breakdown of its mother element, uranium.   We can measure how much lead is in the rock, and because we think we know how fast (or slowly) the uranium would decay into the lead, the amount of this special lead in the rock should then tell us how old the rock is.   In other words, the amount of lead present in the rock would have resulted from a certain amount of uranium decaying over X number of years into lead.   For all of this to yield a specific time frame in millions or billions of years, certain assumptions are made.

ASSUMPTION ONE: NO CONTAMINATION

First, it is assumed by the scientist dating the rock that his specimen of rock had never been contaminated. Nothing could have come into or out of the rock that could alter the dating technique to give an erroneous date. This would demand a "closed system" for the rock's environment. As Dr. Henry Morris says in Scientific Creationism,[95] there is no such thing in nature as a closed system. The closed system is an ideal concept convenient for analysis, but non-existent in the real world. Morris mentions that the idea of a system remaining closed for millions of years becomes an absurdity. Some evolutionists claim that every molecule in the universe has been in at least four different substances since the Big Bang. But evolutionists cannot have both; they cannot have molecules jumping around from one substance to another and molecules steadfast and immovable, as they would have to be in the closed system.

Therefore, the first assumption needed to affix old dates to rocks is not valid. Rocks do get contaminated as things seep into them, and rocks change their constituents as things leech out of them. A closed system sounds good and must be assumed to have accuracy in dating rocks, but it does not occur in nature.

ASSUMPTION TWO: NO DAUGHTER COMPONENT

The second assumption of the rock-dating expert is that the system must have initially contained none of its daughter component. In order to calculate the age of our rock specimen, for example, there can be no lead in the original rock. Let us say it takes 1,000,000 years for one milligram of

---

[95] Dr. Henry Morris, *Scientific Creationism* (San Diego: Creation-Life Pubs., 1974), Chapter VI.

lead to be produced by the decay of uranium. We then analyze a rock and discover it has one milligram of lead in it.

The article we publish would state, with full conviction, "This rock was 1,000,000 years old as scientifically dated using high-tech procedures by Dr. Credentials who has a double Ph.D. in rock dating." Who will doubt how old the rock is? Almost no one. But hold on for a minute. Suppose God created that rock with some of the lead already in it. Or suppose some lead leaked into it somehow or was formed by some other reaction or process. How can the expert differentiate between the lead that God put there (or was formed in some other way) and the lead that came from uranium decay? Obviously, no one can know how much lead was there to begin with. Consequently, for laboratory "accuracy" the evolutionist must arbitrarily decide, "There was no lead (daughter element) there to begin with; I can't prove it, but I will pretend (assume) this to be true."

Every time you are told that a rock is several million or billion or even tens of thousands of years old, the scientist doing the dating has assumed no pre-existing daughter compound. This means he guesses every time. Do we take scientists' guesses as valid fact and then proceed to the belief that the Bible must be wrong when it talks of 24-hour creation days about six thousand years ago? Surely not!

ASSUMPTION THREE: CONSTANT DECAY RATE

The third assumption listed by Dr. Henry Morris (Scientific Creationism, p. 138) is that "The process rate must have always been the same." If the process rate (the speed at which the mother element breaks down into the daughter element) has ever changed since the rock was formed, then the change of rate of decay would have to be corrected for the age calculation to be accurate. Scientists now know that process rates can be altered by various factors. Decay rates can be speeded up or slowed down in certain substances when subjected to various types of radiation and X-rays. As Dr. Morris states, every process in nature operates at a rate which is influenced by a number of different factors (p. 139).

What if radiation bombarded the primitive earth causing the uranium 238 to speed up its decay process (in other words, its half-life was shortened due to the radiation energy). How would the scientist know that the decay process was speeded up during that radiation bombardment one billion years ago? He couldn't know, could he? This means that he could not accurately date the rock. What if the radiation caused the decay rate to speed up, but previous to the x-rays it was twice as slow as it is today? How would the scientist tell us the age of the rock? He could not do it. Yet, have we not been told that a massive bombardment of x-rays hit the primordial ooze of ancient planet earth causing the "spark" that moved dead chemicals into living cells? The so-called "punctuated equilibrium" theory would insist there have been many radiation bombardments over time to cause one kind of animal to rapidly mutate into a higher form. (Punctuated equilibrium teaches that evolution happens too fast to see, in contrast to Darwinian evolution which teaches evolution happens too slow to see.)

It seems that the evolutionists cannot have both. If radiation causes decay rates to speed up or slow down, then the radiation needed to start life from non-life and mutate (change) old life forms into new ones would totally invalidate those billion-year dates and their dating techniques. The atomic clocks would have speeded up or slowed down depending upon the radiation. Let's also look at this the other way around: if there were no radiation bombardments, then the third of the three dating assumptions listed above might even be correct (even though the other two would of themselves destroy the accuracy of the dating technique) -- but now we don't have the radiation "spark" to get life going from non-living chemicals and to stimulate the necessary mutations assumed to improve the organisms! With no radiation, the decay rates may have remained constant for billions of years, but what energy got evolution started and kept it going in this case?

As Dr. Morris says, educated guesses are made to determine apparent ages.   But the apparent age may be completely unrelated to the true age of the rock.

These three assumptions: (1) a closed system, (2) no original daughter element, and (3) the same decay rate throughout all time -- are always involved when a scientist dates a rock. None of these assumptions are valid, and none are able to be subjected to the scientific method of observation and reproducible experimentation. There is no way to accurately date anything beyond several thousand years. That means the earth could be quite young and no scientist can absolutely prove otherwise!

> "...there is certainly no real proof that the vast evolutionary time scale is valid at all.
>
> That being true, there is no compelling reason why we should not seriously consider once again the possibilities in the relatively short time scale of the creation model.
>
> As a matter of fact, the creation model does not, in its basic form, *require* a short time scale. It merely assumes a period of special creation sometime in the past, without necessarily stating when that was. On the other hand, the evolution model does *require* a *long* time scale. The creation model is thus free to consider the evidence on its own merits, whereas the evolution model is forced to reject all evidence that favors a short time scale.
>
> Although the creation model is not necessarily linked to a short time scale, as the evolution model is to a long scale, it is true that it does fit more naturally in a short chronology. Assuming the Creator had a purpose in His creation, and that purpose centered primarily in man, it does seem more appropriate that He would not waste aeons of time in essentially meaningless

caretaking of an incomplete stage or stages of His intended creative work." [96]

The truth is that we have been taught a lie from our earliest school days.[97] We are taught to believe that the earth is very old even though there is no <u>factual</u> science (see Chapter 2 "assumptions") to support aeons of time. But we are not taught the bountiful evidences that lead to the conclusion that the earth is quite possibly only a few thousand years old. How many evidences for a young earth can you list right now? Did you try to think of some? Can you write down even one solid proof that the earth is young? Most people (including Christians) cannot think of even one proof of a young age for the earth. You see, we have been led into one of the lies of Satan's world system -- that the universe is very old. If a group of Christians were asked, "Do you believe God created the heavens and the earth?" Every hand would go up attesting to their sure belief, "Yes, God created the heavens and the earth." Should a second question be proposed, "Do you believe God used billions of years of geologic ages and the process of evolution to create?", some pauses and waffling would occur, and if everyone was being honest, many hands would go up. Now, a third question is in order, "Do you believe that God created the heavens and the earth, the sea and all that is in them in a literal six 24-hour day week? In one evangelical church in Dallas, Texas, only five hands went up in a class of fifty people. You say, "They must not have understood the question!" No, they understood, but only five believed what the Bible says in Genesis 1-11, Exodus 20, John 1,

---

[96] Dr. Henry Morris, *Scientific Creationism*, p. 136.

[97] An in-depth study of the lies and consequences of evolution is Ken Ham's book, *The Lie: Evolution* (El Cajon, CA: Master Books, 1987).

Colossians 1, Hebrews 1, Revelation 4:11, etc. They had been brainwashed by Satan's world system into thinking there is plenty of scientific evidence to prove an old, old universe.

Dr. John C. Whitcomb has done us all a great service with his book, The Early Earth: Revised Edition. Dr. Whitcomb lists and discusses many of the evidences for believing the Bible to be true as written. He contrasts faith in God and His word to faith in evolution and an old earth:

"...the non-Christian scientist must acknowledge that *he also* comes to the factual, observable phenomenon with a set of basic assumptions and presuppositions that reflect a profound "faith-commitment." No scientist in the world today was present when the earth came into existence, nor do any of us have the privilege of watching worlds being created today! Therefore, the testimony of an honest evolutionist could be expressed in terms of ...Hebrews 11:3..., as follows: "By faith, I, an evolutionist, understand that the worlds were *not* framed by the word of any god, so that what is seen has indeed been made out of previously existing and less complex visible things, by purely natural processes, through billions of years." Thus it is not a matter of the *facts* of science versus the *faith* of Christians! The fundamental issue, in the matter of ultimate origins, is whether one puts his trust in the written Word of the personal and living God who *was* there when it all happened, or else puts his trust in the ability of the human intellect, unaided by divine revelation to extrapolate presently observed processes of nature in the eternal past (and future). *Which faith* is the most reasonable, fruitful and satisfying? In my own case, while studying historical geology and paleontology at Princeton University, I was totally committed to evolutionary perspectives. Since then, however, I have discovered the biblical concept of ultimate origins to be far more satisfying in every respect.

Christians who truly desire to honor God in their thinking, must not come to the first Chapter of Genesis with preconceived ideas of what could or could not have happened (in terms of current and changing concepts of uniformitarian scientism). *We are not God's counselors; He is ours! `For who has known the mind of the Lord, or who became His counselor?'* (Romans

11:34) ...For My thoughts are not your thoughts, neither are your ways My ways, saith the Lord. For as the heavens are higher than the earth, so are my ways higher than your ways, and my thoughts than your thoughts' (Isa. 55:8-9)." [98]

Do we know what we believe as Christians? Are we ready to make a defense to everyone who ask us to give an account of the hope that is within us? (I Peter 3:15)

IS EARTH 6 THOUSAND
OR 4.5 BILLION YEARS OLD?

How divergent are these two views (creation and a young earth versus evolution and an old earth)? The Bible places the Beginning at about 6,000 years ago. Many evolutionists put the beginning of earth at about 4 1/2 billion years ago. Dennis Peterson attempts to help us understand the degree of difference in these two choices of faith:

"One way to visualize the extremes of our choices is to equate one year to the thinness of one page from a typical Bible. If you were to stack up several Bibles to a height about equal with your knee, you'd have about 6,000 pages before you.

Now how many Bibles would you have to stack up to make four and a half billion pages?

The stack would reach at least a hundred and fourteen miles high into the stratosphere.

So, you're standing there between your two stacks, and you are supposed to choose which one to believe in. Why is it you are made to feel rather sheepish to admit that you lean toward the Biblical stack of about 6,000 years? Or why is it that you start to arrogantly ridicule anyone who would dare to not agree with your proud billions?" [99]

Petersen lists 35 or 40 evidences for a young earth. These are scientific reasons to believe the universe to be quite

---

[98] Dr. John C. Whitcomb, *The Early Earth: Revised Edition* (Grand Rapids: Baber Book House, 1986), p. 52.

[99] Petersen, *Unlocking the Mysteries of Creation*, Vol. I, p. 34.

young -- on the order of several thousand rather than several billion years. Petersen states:

> "Scientists are aware of over 70 methods that can give us ideas of Earth's age. We could call these "GEOLOGIC CLOCKS." All of them are based on the obvious reality that natural processes occurring steadily through time produce cumulative and often measurable results. Most of these "clocks" give a relatively young age for the Earth. Only a few of them yield a conclusion of billions of years. Those few are loudly publicized to support the commonly held theory of gradualism." [100]

The gravitational fields of the sun and stars pull cosmic dust toward them. This is known as the Poynting-Robertson effect. Our sun is estimated to suck in about 100,000 tons of cosmic dust every day. An old sun should have "pulled in" and destroyed all the particles in our solar system. Yet, our solar system is full of these particles! The Poynting-Robertson effect would demand a sun and solar system of less then 10,000 years of age.[101] Petersen states:

> "All stars have a gravitational field and pull in particles like gas, dust and meteors within their range. Stars radiating energy 100,000 times faster than our sun have a spiraling effect, pulling things in all the faster. The unusual thing is that O and B stars are observed to have huge dust clouds surrounding them. If they

---

[100] Ibid, Petersen, p. 35.

[101] For more about the Poynting Robertson phenomenon, see: R.L. Wysong, *The Creation-Evolution Controversy* (Midland, Mich: Inquiry Press, 1981), p. 454ff. Also: Scott Huse, *The Collapse of Evolution* (Baker Books, 1983), p. 29.

were very old at all, every particle in close range would have been pulled in by now." [102]

Two types of stars have huge dust clouds and, hence, must be quite young. No one has ever seen the birth of a new star, although some scientists have postulated through computer simulations and theoretical mathematics that as many as three new stars should form every year. No scientist ever has, nor ever will see a star form because the Creator created all of His stars on the fourth day of the creation week (Genesis 1:14-19). In the spring of 1992 some scientists claimed to be observing a star form out in the stellar heavens. They used various mathematical equations to come to their conclusion. However, if their conclusion is in direct contradiction to what the Bible says, then their conclusion is wrong. So we sit back and wait a few months or years and finally some scientist will sheepishly admit "We are sorry folks, all our meticulously produced evidence led us to believe a new star was forming, but we now realize that we made a mistake. We will keep looking for a new star to form and we will let you know as soon as we find it." God created His last star out of nothing on the fourth day of the creation week!

Astronomers may see stars die since entropy and sin entered the universe, but no star-birth is possible; God completed His creation of the universe and rested on the seventh day. If a star (O and B) and/or a solar system (ours) has significant cosmic dust and meteoroids in the space around it, it cannot be billions of years old.

---

[102] Ibid, Petersen, p. 44.

LIGHT FROM THE FARTHEST STARS

You might be thinking, "Okay, but what about the speed of light and the millions of years necessary to get light from the farthest stars to our solar system?" (This is one of the things I was thinking as I was "evolving" into a creationist back in the early seventies.) Well, first of all, how do we know it takes millions of years for light to travel to earth from the farthest stars? Some evolutionary professor told us, or some writer told us, or someone like Walter Cronkite or Dan Rather or Carl Sagan told us. There does seem to be a problem here, doesn't there? What if you were to discover that light from the farthest star could arrive at earth instantly (God created the star and the light beams from the star to the earth. We can't eliminate this possibility. Our God could do this if He wanted to) or within three days?

Dr. Barry Setterfield has done considerable work on this problem. His papers can be obtained through the Institute for Creation Research, Box 1607, El Cajon, CA 92022. Also see I.C.R. Impact #121, <u>Starlight and the Age of the Universe</u>, by Richard Niessen. Setterfield and Niessen offer four possible solutions to the problem of light from the farthest stars. The first possibility is that God could create the light beam with the appearance of age. A second possibility is that the distance to these remote stars has not been calculated correctly. This is very likely when the methods used to measure great distances in space are closely examined in conjunction with the basic assumptions of Trigonometry. As I.C.R. Impact #121 states, "There is no guarantee that actual distances in space are as great as we have been told." Once you get out of our solar system it is a most difficult problem to accurately measure distance.

A third consideration is that light may have taken a "shortcut" through space. Different types of mathematics and different assumptions and postulates give totally different concepts of space and distances in space. What we know about space is quite limited. How distances through space are calculated depends on the calculator's system of math and his or her basic set of postulates (assumptions).

Outer space may be straight or it may be curved. If you like to think outer space is a straight line, you will use Euclidean Geometry and its accompanying assumptions. Euclidean Geometry is used to find vast distances in space. Its calculations are, for the most part, straight line calculations.

But what if outer space is not able to be measured with straight line from here-to-there-type math? That would mean all the farthest stars could be much closer than the textbooks teach.

NON-EUCLIDEAN GEOMETRY

Another legitimate way to measure distances in outer space is by using Riemannian math. Riemannian math is classified as Non-Euclidean Geometry. It assumes outer space to be curved. Hence Non-Euclidean Geometry produces much smaller distances to the farthest stars. Niessen (I.C.R. Impact #121) reviewed articles by Harold Slusher ("Age of the Cosmos" I.C.R. 1980) and Wayne Zage ("The Geometry of Binocular Visual Space", Mathematics Magazine 53, Nov. 1980, pp. 289-293). Twenty-seven binary star systems were observed, and it appears that light travels in curved paths in deep space. If you convert Euclidean straight line math into Riemannian curved math, light could travel from the farthest stars to earth in, as reported by Niessen, 15.71 years! This is a whole lot less than millions of years, isn't it?

Is Riemannian Geometry valid if it shows shorter distances to the stars? H.S.M. Coxeter published a largely ignored book in 1942 entitled Non-Euclidean Geometry.

Coxeter stated, "...we still can't decide whether the real world is approximately Euclidean or approximately non-Euclidean." [103] The scientists do not know which is the valid way to measure space as it really is! They are not sure just what outer space really looks like. They have not been there and do not know what shape it has. Everything close enough to our solar system to obtain measurements (though all these contain assumptions) appears to have positive curvature. That means Riemann's method of figuring distance in space is more likely to be correct than the Euclidean methods. Niessen, then, has a better than average chance of being correct when he postulates 15.71 years for light from the farthest star to reach planet earth.

THE SPEED OF LIGHT

---

[103] "The full recognition that spherical geometry is itself a kind of non-Euclidean geometry, without parallels, is due to Riemann (1826-1866). He realized that Saccheri's hypothesis of the obtuse angle becomes valid as soon as Postulates I,II, and V are modified to read:

I. *Any two points determine at least one line.*

II. *A line is unbounded.*

V. *Any two lines in a plane will meet.*

For a line to be unbounded and yet of finite length, it merely has to be re-entrant, like a circle. The great circles on a sphere provide a model for the finite lines on a finite plane, and, when so interpreted, satisfy the modified postulates. But if a line and a plane can each be finite and yet unbounded, why not also an *n*-dimensional manifold, and in particular the three-dimensional space of the real world? In Riemann's words of 1854: "The unboundedness of space possesses a greater empirical certainty than any external experience. But its infinite extent by no means follows
from this; on the other hand, if we assume independence of bodies from position, and therefore ascribe to space constant curvature, it must necessarily be finite provided this curvature has ever so small a positive value."

According to the General Theory of Relativity, astronomical space has positive curvature locally (wherever there is matter), but we cannot tell whether the curvature of "empty" space is exactly zero or has a very small positive or negative value. In other words, we still cannot decide whether the real world is approximately Euclidean or approximately non-Euclidean." H. S. M. Coxeter, *Non-Euclidean Geometry*, 5th ed. (Canada: University of Toronto Press, 1965), pp. 11,12.

Niessen adds one more factor: the speed of light. Scientists have been measuring the speed of light for over 300 years, and it is appears to be slowing down. Using equations to extrapolate backwards, equations that include the figures observed and registered for the slowing down of the speed of light (the farther back in time you go the faster the light travels), light from a five billion light-year away star (assuming stars are that far away) could arrive on earth in just <u>three</u> days!

What conclusion can we arrive at on the basis of the above? You do not have to believe it when some textbook or scientist in a white lab coat tells you that stars are millions of light-years and perhaps trillions of miles away. There is no hard, <u>irrefutable</u> evidence here for a 9 to 20 billion year old universe.

Where do the 9 to 20 billion years come from? A man named Hubble (remember "Hubble's telescope" launched into space recently?) came up with the theoretical, mathematical formula for measuring time back to the initial "Big Bang". His calculations originally estimated about 18 to 20 billion years as the age of the universe. Then a few years ago, some other scientists decided Hubble had made a grievous mistake and was 50% off in his calculations. Thus, the age of the universe was cut in half (from 18 to 20 billion years to 9 to 10 billion years) by the stroke of pen. Some scientists still hold to the 20 billion year figure. They realize that even 20 billion years is statistically not long enough to evolve the universe.

COMBUSTION ENERGY OF STARS

Now, back to some more evidences for a young earth. Astronomers calculate that "O" and "B" stars may have surface temperatures of 90,000°F. This is "... more than 100,000 times the energy coming from our sun. Burning down at that rate, and clocking backward, the entire universe would have been filled with the mass of these stars just a few thousand years ago!" [104]

Some evolutionists will object, "But you can't take current processes and extrapolate back like that." Well, what do evolutionists do to find and publish their old, old dates? The same thing!   They evaluate, for example, present processes such as decay rates (l/2 life), and extrapolate backwards assuming all was the same from the beginning (II Peter 3).

BRISTLE-CONE PINE TREES

If the Biblical Flood occurred about 5,000 years ago and destroyed all dry-land plant life, then we would not expect to find plants that could be accurately dated at older than about 5,000 years. The bristle-cone pine tree is such a plant. It has been called the oldest living organism on earth and has been accurately dated at about 5,000 years. Peterson states, "It's almost as though all these trees were planted on a virgin Earth just 5,000 years ago." [105]

RIVERS ARE YOUNG

Every year the Mississippi River carries tons and tons of eroded dirt into the Gulf of Mexico. Scientists have been measuring the growth of the Mississippi delta for many years.

"At the present rate **the entire Mississippi River delta would have accumulated in only 5,000 years**. But science acknowledges that the river has been even bigger in the past.

---

[104] Petersen, p. 44.
[105] Ibid, p. 38.

How could this be? Unless of course the North American continent, and all the other continents for that matter, just haven't been in their present positions any longer than that." [106]

Another river that scientists carefully watch is the Niagara. It also leads to belief in a young earth.

"Because the rim of the falls is wearing back at a known rate every year, geologists recognize that is has only taken about 5,000 years to erode from its original precipice." [107]

Often large chunks of the dirt and rock under water falls, like the Niagara, will break off, yielding even younger ages. Suppose that 200 years from now you decided to calculate the age of Niagara Falls, but you did not know that in 1994 a huge section of rock had broken away from the edge of the falls. You would assume that it took thousands of years to wear away all that rock from the falls' edge, but it happened in an instant. You would date the falls much older than it actually was.   This type of mistake is common when scientists attempt to date things.

THE RECEDING MOON

Adding to the evidence for a young earth is our receding moon. Scientists know how fast our moon is moving away from earth (about two inches per year).

Louis B. Slichter, Professor of Geophysics at M.I.T., writes:

---

[106] Ibid, p. 38.
[107] Ibid, p. 39.

"The time scale of the earth-moon system still presents a major problem." [108]

Dennis Petersen continues:

"...working it back would mean the moon and Earth would be touching only two billion years ago. Of course, that's ridiculous. Another way to look at it is this: At the present rate and starting from a realistic distance of separation between the two, if the Earth is five billion years old the moon should be out of sight by now!" [109]

MOON ROCKS

When the first moon rocks were dated in the early 1970's, NASA published the age of the moon rocks at 4 to 4.5 billion years. Several years and many rocks later, they published a range of dates for the rocks of our moon at 3 to 4 1/2 billion years. This author called one of the geologists who dated those rocks and the conversation went something like this:

"I noticed in a recent news release that the dates of the moon rocks have been adjusted to a range of 1 1/2 billion years. That's a pretty big difference in the dates! Was the range any greater than that?"

"Oh yes, the range went from several thousand years to over 20 billion years."

"Well then, why did NASA only publish the 1 1/2 billion year range, instead of the full 20+ billion year range?"

"We did not want to confuse the public. We know the moon is about 3 to 4 1/2 billion years old, so we called the dates outside of that range discordant dates and threw them out."

Apparently, some scientists have pre-decided that the moon is about 3 to 4 1/2 billion years old. What if, in spite of their presuppositional belief, the several thousand year

---

[108] Louis B. Slichter, "Secular Effects of Tidal Friction upon the Earth's Rotation," *Journal of Geophysical Research*, Vol. 8 No. 14 (1964), 4281-4288.

[109] Petersen, p. 43.

dates were correct and not discordant? Well, that locks in Special Creation and eliminates the possibility of evolution (which <u>requires</u> millions of years). Apparently that would be unacceptable to NASA. Or, what if the 20+ billion dates were correct? That, in effect, demolishes Hubble's math, and the time of the Big Bang is once again up for grabs. These scientists might object and say, "But we use a bell-shaped curve to arrive at our dates." Well, what if the assumptions which are built into their dating system skew the curve one way or another? We've already seen that the three major assumptions invariably included when scientists date rocks (earlier in this chapter) are not valid.

You might ask an astronomer where our moon and its rocks came from. Some fanciful answers will be forthcoming! Evolutionary scientists do not know from whence cometh our moon. A creationist believes that the God of the Bible created the moon, and the sun and stars as well, on the fourth day of the creation week (Genesis 1:14-19). There is no hard, factual, scientific information that can refute a young age for the moon. All old ages given for the moon are not accurate because the assumptions of the dating techniques do not square with reality.

SHORT-TERM COMETS

From time to time, comets pass by the earth. Not only can scientists not tell us where our moon came from, they also cannot tell us about the origin of short-term comets. These are comets that astronomers calculate have lifetimes of no more than 10,000 years. If the universe is somewhere between 9 and 20 billion years old, and the astral bodies were formed at the "Big Bang", evolution is left in the embarrassing dilemma of having to postulate theories for the origin of short-term comets, which it cannot prove. You have to admire the imagination of these folks, though. Some actually believe that Jupiter spits comets out of high volcanoes. The only problem is that the short-lived comets are not made of the right stuff to come from Jupiter, and their orbit is in no way oriented to enable them to refer to Jupiter as "mother". Scott Huse says:

> "Comets journey around the sun and are assumed to be the same age as the solar system. Each time a comet orbits the sun, a small part of its mass is `boiled off`. Careful studies indicate that the effect of this dissolution process on short-term comets would have totally dissipated them in about 10,000 years. Based on the fact that there are still numerous comets orbiting the sun with no source of new comets known to exist, we can deduce that our solar system cannot be much older than 10,000 years. To date, no satisfactory explanation has been given to discredit this evidence for a youthful solar system." [110]

EARTH'S MAGNETIC FIELD

An examination of the Earth's magnetic field proves that Earth cannot be very old, since the Earth's magnetic field is losing its strength. Dr. Thomas Barnes has done volumes of work on the depletion of Earth's magnetic field. The conclusion of his work establishes the age of the Earth at less than 10,000 years.[111] Naturally, the evolutionary community has proclaimed Barnes' work invalid, but Barnes answers their charges quite simply and effectively in the ICR Impact #122 of August 1983 entitled Earth's Magnetic Age: The Achilles Heel of Evolution. The earth's magnetic field is

---

[110] Huse, *The Collapse of Evolution*, pp. 28,29.

[111] For more see: *Origin and Destiny of the Earth's Magnetic Field*, T.G. Barnes, I.C.R. Technical Monograph No. 4, 1973; also I.C.R. Impact #100, October 1981.

getting measurably weaker. Ten thousand years ago it would have been too strong to support life. If life could not have existed 10,000 years ago because of the super-strength of the earth's magnetic field, then evolution had no time to occur.

OUR SHRINKING SUN

Recently a controversy has arisen over the shrinking of our sun. If the figures of John Eddy and Adam Boornazian are correct ("Analysis of Historical Data Suggest the Sun is Shrinking," Physics Today, Vol. 32 No. 9, September 1979), our sun would have been too hot for life to exist on Earth even 1,000,000 years ago. This would, in effect, knock out the possibility of the vast expanses of time required for evolution. Evolutionists and theistic evolutionists have jumped on this one to prove Eddy was mistaken. Others now claim the measurements of the planet Mercury crossing in front of the sun each year, prove the size of the sun has not changed. We will have to wait to see how this develops.[112]

RADIOHALOS

Irrefutable support for a young earth is offered by Robert V. Gentry through his studies of radiohalos in coalified

---

[112] *Science Held Hostage* is a book by three men from Calvin College who appear to be theistic evolutionists. They do not believe in a young earth. The "evolution/creation in six days" controversy is not an issue to cause the elect to lose fellowship with each other. (Howard J. Van Till, Davis A. Young and Clarence Menninga, *Science Held Hostage*(Downers Grove, Ill: Inter Varsity Press, 1988). Theodore Rybka in his book, Geophysical and Astronomical Clocks (American Writing and Publishing Co.: Irvine, CA, 1993) refutes the arguments of Hugh Ross and Van Till, Young and Menninga by showing that the sun's heat is generated by gravitational collapse and not nuclear fusion.

wood.[113]   Evolutionists believe the coal deposits in the Colorado Plateau to be hundreds of millions of years old. Yet, Gentry's radio-halo "clock" demands a time period of only a few thousand years.

Gentry discovered microscopic bits of uranium in these coal deposits. The effect of the radioactive uranium on the coal was to produce radiation halos in the coal.

> "As a radioactive bit decays, radiation extends in all directions into surrounding coal for a small, yet precise distance determined by the particle energy of the radiation. Over time this emitted radiation will change the color of the coal, forming a distinct sphere around the bit of uranium in the center. These tiny spheres of discolored rock surrounding a microscopic radioactive center are termed "radiohalos".   Such radiohalos are Robert Gentry's specialty." [114]

How does the bit of radioactive uranium get into the coal to form the halos? Ackerman continues:

> "Regarding the radioactive center, a bit of uranium has, at some time in the past, before the wood material was hardened into coal, migrated into its present position. As the uranium bit undergoes radioactive decay, a form of lead is created. Once the coal has hardened and the uranium bit has been cemented into a fixed position, this lead isotope begins to accumulate at the site....
> Gentry has found that the uranium/lead ratios in the Colorado Plateau coal formation indicate that this formation is only a few thousand years old." [115]

---

[113] Robert V. Gentry, et al., " Radiohalos in Coalified Wood: New Evidence Relating to the Time of Uranium Introduction and Coalification," *Science*, 194 (October 15, 1976), 315-317.

[114] Paul D. Ackerman, *It's a Young World After All: Exciting Evidences for Recent Creation* (Grand Rapids: Baker Book House, 1986), pp. 104,105.

[115] Ibid, Ackerman,p. 105.

The halos form around the radioactive particles in the coal and indicate a young age of only a few thousand years for the coal. The coal of the Colorado Plateau was probably formed during the Flood judgment of Noah's day as God was destroying heaven and earth system #1.

Gentry also found halos of Polonium in Precambrian granite rock. These are supposedly the oldest rocks on earth. Precambrian rock is called the "basement" rock of earth since it is thought to be more ancient than all other rock. Ackerman reviews Gentry's work:

"The question Gentry has raised for evolutionists is how the polonium bits and their resulting halos came to be in the basement granites....

The enigma is this: If the granite is hardened, the polonium cannot travel to its intrusion location. But if the granite is not hardened, no halo can form. Therefore, Gentry argues that the time lapse from a permeable, molten state to the present rock state for these precambrian granites had to be extremely brief. How brief? One of the polonium isotopes studies by Gentry has a half-life of three minutes! Another has a half-life of only 164 microseconds!

In the evolutionary model, the time required for the cooling and solidification of these granites is millions and millions of years. Gentry believes these halos to constitute powerful evidence against evolution and its presumed vast time spans. He believes these halos speak of a very rapid formation of these crustal rocks." [116]

Radiohalos in Precambrian basement rock may indicate a young age for the earth's "oldest" rocks. Walter T. Brown, Jr., (In The Beginning), lists about thirty time clocks for the age of the earth that yield an age of a few thousand years. He mentions that an analysis of the gases (such as helium) in the atmosphere yields a young age (few thousand years) for the age of the atmosphere.[117] River sediments and erosion

---

[116] Ibid, Ackerman, pp. 108-110.

[117] Brown, *In the Beginning*, p. 16.

rates indicate that the earth could not have existed as it is for millions of years.[118]

PLANETARY RINGS

A study of the rings around several planets seems to demand a young age for our solar system:

> "The rings that are orbiting Saturn, Uranus, Jupiter and Neptune are being rapidly bombarded by meteoroids. Saturn's rings, for example, should be pulverized and dispersed in about 10,000 years. Since this has not happened, planetary rings are probably quite young...
>
> Jupiter and Saturn each radiate more than twice the energy they receive from the sun. Venus also radiates too much energy. Calculations show it is very unlikely that this energy comes from nuclear fusion, radioactive decay, gravitational contraction or phase changes within those planets. The only other conceivable explanation is that these planets have not existed long enough to cool off." [119]

STAR CLUSTERS

The existence of star clusters hints at a young universe. Immense clusters of stars are travelling through space at supersonic speeds. Scientists believe that gravity holds these fast moving star clusters together. But scientists do not know how these star clusters could hold together for millions of years, while travelling at such high speeds. They should have "unclustered" and moved apart by now. But they are still in a cluster. The sole answer to this dilemma for the evolutionist appears to be special creation a few thousand years ago, not a "Big Bang" billions of years ago.

---

[118] Ibid, Brown, p. 16.
[119] Ibid, p. 18.

MOUNT ST. HELENS

When all other evidence fails to prove a very old heaven and earth system, evolutionists go back to rocks and rock formations, which supposedly require very long spans of time to form. The eruption of Mount St. Helens on May 18, 1980, and the rapid formation of geologic systems around it is challenging the claims of historical geology. Dr. Steve Austin and Institute for Creation Research staff personnel have been documenting the phenomena of Mount St. Helens since its initial eruption. Some surprising results of the volcanic blast are being observed.

> "Up to 600 feet thickness of strata have formed since 1980 at Mount St. Helens. These deposits accumulated from primary air blast, landslide, waves on the lake, pyroclastic flows, mud flows, air fall and stream water... Mount St. Helens teaches us that the stratified layers commonly characterizing geological formations can form very rapidly by flow processes." [120]

In other words, what geologists may have thought took thousands or hundreds of thousands of years to form as a column of rock in fact formed at Mount St. Helens as the scientists watched, and in less than eleven years! Perhaps aeons of time are not necessary to form the layers of rock after all.

One more fascinating phenomenon of the Mount St. Helens cataclysmic explosion is the apparent formation of the beginnings of polystrate fossils in five years. In 1985, scientists discovered that water-soaked trees were floating with root end down (toward the bottom of the lake) in Spirit Lake. These trees:

---

[120] Steven A. Austin, Ph.D., "Mount St. Helens and Catastrophism," ICR Impact #157, July 1986, p. 1,2. Dr. Austin also has an excellent video on this topic.

"...are randomly spaced not clumped together, over the bottom of the lake, again having the appearance of being an <u>in situ</u> forest.

Scuba investigation of the upright deposited trunks shows that some are already solidly buried by sedimentation, with more than three feet of sediment around their bases. This proved that the upright trees were deposited at different times, with their roots buried at different levels. If found buried in the stratigraphic record (rocks), these trees might be interpreted as multiple forests which grew on different levels over periods of thousands of years. The Spirit Lake upright deposited stumps, therefore, have considerable implications for interpreting "petrified forests" in the stratigraphic record." [121]

What does this all mean? There is a bank of polystrata fossils (one tree goes up through several layers or strata of sedimentary rock) in Nova Scotia over 2,000 feet thick with trees straight up and down at different levels up through the rocks. Geologists have claimed that a formation like the Nova Scotia formation would take hundreds of thousands of years to form. After observing the Spirit Lake water-soaked trees, scientists are reconsidering. Perhaps it does not take as long as they originally thought to form polystrate fossils. Those trees in Spirit Lake are lining up and getting buried in what should become sedimentary rock -- but less than fourteen years have gone by, not hundreds of thousands of years!

With the many evidences for a young earth, evidences which can only be answered with an earth that once was greenhouse warm and suddenly (at the Flood) became permanently frozen at the poles, why do evolutionists still cling to their theories? Only one answer seems plausible: they do not want to submit themselves in humble obedience

---

[121] Austin, ICR Impact #157, p. iii.

to their Creator. They refuse to accept God even though He reveals Himself through His creation. Evolution from one cell to man is a lie and a foolish speculation of men in rebellion against their Creator.

"For the wrath of God is revealed from heaven against all ungodliness and unrighteousness of men, who hold the truth in unrighteousness;

Because that which may be known of God is manifest in them; for God hath shewed it to them.

For the invisible things of him from the creation of the world are clearly seen, being understood by the things that are made, even his eternal power and divine Godhead; so that they are without excuse.

<u>Because that, when they knew God, they glorified *him* not as God, neither were thankful; but became vain in their imaginations, and their foolish heart was darkened</u>.

Professing themselves to be wise, they became fools."
Romans 1:18-22 (Emphasis added)

MARVEL OF GOD'S CREATION #10
The Woodpecker

If there is any animal that breaks the rules of evolution in such a way that it could not possibly have evolved, then it would need God as its Creator. The woodpecker is an example of such an animal.

The woodpecker's beak is unlike that of other birds. It is designed to hammer its way into the hardest of trees. If the woodpecker evolved, how would it develop its thick, tough beak? Let's suppose some bird decided that there must be all kinds of little critters which would be good for lunch hidden beneath the bark of trees. This bird decided to peck through the bark and into the hardwood tree. On first peck this bird discovered problems with the way it was put together. Its beak shattered when it was slammed against the tree, its tail feathers broke, and it developed a migraine-strength headache.

With a shattered beak, the little bird was unable to eat and so it died. Now this bird began to think, "I must evolve a thicker beak and stronger tail feathers and something to help prevent headaches." Of course not. Dead animals can not evolve anything. Yet the woodpecker not only has an industrial-strength beak, it also has a special cartilage between its head and beak to absorb some of the shock from the continuous drumming. Woodpeckers go home at night without a headache.

To help with the absorption of the constant pounding, the woodpecker has uniquely resilient tail feathers. It uses its tail feathers and feet to form a tripod effect as it clings to the tree. Even its feet are specially designed to enable it to move up, down, and around, vertical tree trunks. The feet of the woodpecker have two toes in front and two toes in back. Most other birds have three toes in front and one in back.

> "This two-plus-two toe pattern....along with stiff yet elastic tail feathers, allows a woodpecker to grasp a tree firmly and balance itself on a vertical surface. When the woodpecker braces itself to chisel a hole, the tail feathers bend and spread, buttressing the bird against the rough tree surface. In this way feet and tail form an effective tripod to stabilize the blows of hammering into wood." [122]

Suppose that somehow a bird, knowing there was lunch in those trees, developed the strong beak, the shock absorber cartilage between the beak and the skull, the ability to move its head faster than you can tap fingers, the "two-plus-two" feet and the super stiff yet elastic tail feathers. This bird still has a major problem. It will starve to death. How could it drag its lunch out of the little insect tunnels in the tree? Have you ever attempted to drag an insect larva out of a tunnel? They hang on!

God has taken care of the woodpecker by creating in it a tongue that is several times longer than the average bird's tongue. Lester and Bohlin comment:

> "...the tongue of a woodpecker is in a class by itself. When chiseling into a tree, the woodpecker will occasionally come across insect tunnels. Its tongue is long and slender and is used to probe these tunnels for insects. The tip is like a spearhead with a number of barbs or hairs pointing rearward. This facilitates securing the insect while transporting it to the beak. A sticky gluelike substance coats the tongue to aid in this process as well." [123]

---

[122] Lane P. Lester and Raymond G. Bohlin, *The Natural Limits to Biological Change* (Grand Rapids: Zondervan, 1984), p. 24.

[123] Ibid, p. 24.

What a fascinating creation!   Not only does the woodpecker have little barbs on the tip of its tongue, it is also a mini glue factory.   And the glue sticks securely to insects but does not stick to the beak of the woodpecker.   Aren't God's creations marvelous!

But this is not all. Most birds have a tongue and a beak about the same length. The tongue of the woodpecker has evolutionists scratching their heads. It can be stretched far beyond the tip of the woodpecker's beak as it searches the larval tunnels for food. The animal kingdom displays no other tongues quite like that of the woodpecker. The tongue of some woodpeckers does not come from its throat up into its mouth like other creatures.   The European Green woodpecker's tongue goes down the throat, out the back of the neck "...around the back of the skull beneath the skin, and over the top between the eyes, terminating usually just below the eye socket." [124]   In some woodpeckers the tongue exits the skull between the eyes and enters the beak through one of the nostrils! How would this evolve? And from what ancestor did the woodpecker inherit its special beak, feet, tail feathers, shock absorbing cartilage, thicker skull and unique tongue?

The woodpecker displays the glory of his Creator who is also our Creator. Why would an evolutionist study a marvel of God's creation such as the woodpecker and still refuse to believe in God the Creator? Only one answer seems to make sense! Pride! Pride! Pride! "Rational," humanistic man thinks that he himself is the "...master of his fate and the captain of his soul...." This blinding pride does not allow the intrusion of a personal sovereign God, but rather sees man as the pinnacle of all that is. The time has come for us to

---

[124] Ibid, p. 25.

humble ourselves and bow before our infinitely righteous Creator!

II Chronicles 7:14, 15 reads:

> If my people, which are called by my name, shall humble themselves and pray, and seek My face, and turn from their wicked ways; then will I hear from heaven, and will forgive their sin, and will heal their land.
>
> Now mine eyes shall be open, and mine ears attent unto the prayer *that is made* in this place.

I Peter 5:5b-7 reads:

> Yea, all *of you*, be subject to one another, and be clothed with humility: for God resisteth the proud, and giveth grace to the humble.
>
> Humble yourselves therefore under the mighty hand of God, that he may exalt you in due time:
>
> Casting all your care upon him; for he careth for you.

Philippians 2:3-11 reads:

> Let nothing *be done* through strife or vainglory; but in lowliness of mind let each esteem the other better than themselves.
>
> Look not every man on his own things, but every man also on the things of others.
>
> Let this mind be in you, which was also in Christ Jesus:
>
> Who, being in the form of God, thought it not robbery to be equal with God:
>
> But made himself of no reputation, and took upon him the form of a servant, and was made in the likeness of men:
>
> And being found in fashion as a man, he humbled himself, and became obedient unto death, even the death of the cross.
>
> Wherefore God also hath highly exalted him, and given him a name which is above every name:
>
> That at the name of Jesus every knee should bow, of *things* in heaven, and *things* in earth, and *things* under the earth;

And that every tongue should confess that Jesus Christ *is* **Lord, to the glory of God the Father.**

Prayer

Have mercy upon me, O God, according to thy lovingkindness; according unto the multitude of thy tender mercies blot out my transgressions. Wash me thoroughly from mine iniquity, and cleanse me from my sin. For I acknowledge my transgressions: and my sin is ever before me. Against thee, thee only, have I sinned, and done this evil in thy sight: that thou mightest be justified when thou speakest, and be clear when thou judgest...Purge me with hyssop, and I shall be clean: wash me, and I shall be whiter than snow. Make me to hear joy and gladness; that the bones which thou has broken may rejoice. Hide thy face from my sins, and blot out all mine iniquities. Create in me a clean heart, O God...(Psalm 51:1-4, 7-10a).

Blessed be the God and Father of our Lord Jesus Christ, who hath blessed me with all spiritual blessings in heavenly places in Christ: According as he hath chose me in him before the foundation of the world, that I should be holy and without blame before him in love: Having predestinated me unto the adoption of children by Jesus Christ to himself, according to the good pleasure of his will, To the praise of the glory of his grace, wherein he hath made me accepted in the beloved. In whom I have redemption through his blood, the forgiveness of sins, according to the riches of his grace. Ephesians 1:3-7, (personal application paraphrase)

Lord Jesus, I believe in You as my Lord and Savior. Help me to walk worthy of You unto all pleasing, being fruitful in every good work, and increasing in the knowledge of God (from Colossians 1:10).

CONCLUSION

You do not have to throw out your brains or any true, scientifically testable and verifiable science to believe in a literal, six, 24-hour day creation that took place approximately six thousand years ago. We can believe that the Creator, the Lord and Savior Jesus Christ, created everything with the appearance of age. He displayed His ability to act without the human necessity of time by His miracles. Science that "proves" billions of years is based on many insupportable and unreasonable assumptions. So we can believe the Bible as it addresses origins even though it does not tell us everything. If certain types of "science" contradict the Scriptures, we can be certain that these "sciences" are either mistaken or misinterpreted or misunderstood -- because the Scriptures are eternal truth.

Evolutionists admit to each other that "...the creationists have the better argument." This is because what we see in life and in the fossils does not display emerging kinds of plants or animals. Evolution from one cell to man is not scientifically observable at all.

The universe is young - on the order of several thousand, not billions, of years old. Man, dinosaur and mastodon walked the earth at the same time. The missing links are missing! God created discrete plants and animals in the Beginning and, with minor variations, these are what we see today. Mutations in the genes do not generate new life forms or even improve present life forms. Mutations harm or kill the organism into which they come. Prehistoric man was either ape, monkey or man and not some genetically evolving apelike man or manlike ape.

The religious quest to prove evolution from the Big Bang to man will occupy the singular life of many, but will end in despair for all who pursue this myth of evolutionary faith.

Macroevolution is the attempt to answer the big questions "How did I get here?" "Who am I?" and "Where am I going?" without belief in God. God Himself says:

> "The fool hath said in his heart, *There is* no God." (Ps. 14:1)
> "Beware lest any man spoil you through philosophy and vain deceit, after the tradition of men, after the rudiments of the world, and not after Christ." (Colossians 2:8)
> "Thus saith the Lord; Cursed be the man trusteth in man, and maketh flesh his arm, and whose heart departeth from the Lord." (Jeremiah 17:5)
> "O Lord, I know that the way of man is not in himself: it is not in man that walketh to direct his steps." (Jeremiah 10:23).
> "There is a way which seemeth right unto a man, but the end thereof are the ways of death." (Proverbs 14:12)

The conflict that started in Genesis 3 still rages today for the hearts and minds of people, yet the battle has already been won at the cross of Calvary.

> "But God commendeth his love toward us, in that, while we were yet sinners, Christ died for us." (Romans 5:8)
> "That if thou shalt confess with thy mouth the Lord Jesus, and shalt believe in thine heart that God hath raised Him from the dead, thou shalt be saved." (Romans 10:9).

Psalm 1 tells us there are only two ways to walk in this world....on the path of the wicked, or the way of the righteous. God has revealed Himself in Creation and through the written Word as the "right way". We will all some day stand before Him to answer for our lives lived in this world, and whether they have been lived for His eternal glory and praise, or for the praise of the power and glory of this world. Since the fall of Genesis 3, man has been more interested in the approval of men, rather than the approval of God (John 5:44; 12:43).

Even as "professing Christians", we have become a people who call **"evil good, and good evil"** (Isa. 5:20).

More than anything else in these deceptive times in which we live, we have allowed ourselves to be **"corrupted from the simplicity that is in Christ" (II Cor. 11:3)**. We have not brought **"...into captivity every thought to the obedience of Christ" (II Cor. 10:5)**. My challenge to Christian and non-Christian is to re-examine where our faith is actually invested. Is it possible that we have been seduced by the world's convincing "arguments of academia", impressive credentials and the ensuing "success", power and prominence that come from finding truth apart from God's Word? His Word is truth (John 17:17), it is eternal, living and active (Heb. 4:12) and, will not return void (Isa. 55:11).

The non-verifiable "assumptions" of the scientific community are accepted without question in our hi-tech, sophisticated, humanistic, impersonal "politically correct" society....even by the majority of professing Christians who hide behind the hypocrisy of being "theistic evolutionists." (Say the theistic evolutionists: Yes, I'll acknowledge that there is a God, but He's not powerful enough to do anything other than to set the wheels in motion and rest on His laurels!) If professing Christians were in God's Word as much, or more than we are in the secular world's beliefs, then we would afford ourselves the opportunity to grow in the grace and knowledge of God's ways and to have the empowerment of the Holy Spirit to lead us into all understanding. I Cor. 3:18, 19B states: **"Let no man deceive himself. If any man among you seemeth to be wise in this world, let him become a fool, that he may be wise. For the wisdom of this world is foolishness with God."**

The bottom line always comes back to faith. Are we going to believe by faith in eternal matter and energy, or eternal God? We all live by faith in one system or the other. No man can reason his way to saving faith in God because God is infinite and we are finite, He is the creator and we are the created. There is a great chasm caused by sin that separates the all-powerful God and Creator of the universe from His fallen creatures: us! When we refuse to accept our position under God in His creation (pride and rebellion), then we tend to look for comfortable alternatives. These alternatives allow us to escape from being created in the image of God and to being responsible to Him, to the independence from God that will ultimately result in death and eternal separation from Him.

Many times creationists are accused of trying to "discredit science" or scientists, an accusation which simply is not true. "Origins Science", as we know it, is based on many assumptions, which by definition are not able to be proved. Assumptions become "truth" when the credentialed, powerful people of the world's system arrange data, and "logically" argue their case while the "Christian" community stands by either accepting (they don't know what the Bible says), or defaulting in that they don't have enough conviction to study the data and speak out for a creationist interpretation of factual science.

The greatest truth that can ever be realized in this life is that Christ died for sinners, and that God gave His only begotten son to accomplish that act of love. Whether we are an unbelieving evolutionist, theistic evolutionist, or creationist is not the main issue. The issue is to whom we have bowed for our eternal destiny....only pride and rebellion will keep us from enjoying that eternal rest in our Creator/Savior's complete forgiveness. Our Lord says to us in Matthew 11:28-30: **"Come unto me, all ye that labour and are heavy laden, and I will give you rest. Take my yoke upon you, and learn of me; for I am meek and lowly in heart: and ye shall find rest unto your souls. For my yoke is easy, and my burden is light."**

"For God so loved the world, that he gave his only begotten Son, that whosoever believeth in him should not perish, but have everlasting life." (John 3:16)

"...Lo, I am with you always, even unto the end of the world. Amen."

SCRIPTURE INDEX

INDEX OF AUTHORS

SUBJECT INDEX

This book is available from:

Biblical Discipleship Publishers
2212 Chisolm Trail
Rockwall, Texas   75087
(214) 771-0568